Leigh Montville

Simon & Schuster New York London Toronto Sydney Tokyo Singapore

MANUTE

The Center of
Two Worlds

SIMON & SCHUSTER
Simon & Schuster Building
Rockefeller Center
1230 Avenue of the Americas
New York, New York 10020

Designed by Hyun Joo Kim
Manufactured in the United States of America

1   3   5   7   9   10   8   6   4   2

Library of Congress Cataloging-in-Publication Data
Montville, Leigh.
Manute: the center of two worlds/Leigh Montville.
p.   cm.
1. Bol, Manute. 2. Basketball players—Biography. I. Title.
GV884.B65M66   1993
796.323′092—dc20
[B]   92–38428
CIP
ISBN 978-1-4516-2072-6

Photo Credits

© Fred Burnham, 11; Courtesy of Frank Catapano, 8; Courtesy of the
Golden State Warriors, 9; Ed Mahan Photo/Courtesy of the Philadelphia
76ers, 10; Manny Millan/*Sports Illustrated*, 6; George Tiedemann/
Sports Illustrated, 12; Courtesy of the University of Bridgeport, 4, 5.
Color spread: © 1992 Brad Trent.

For Robin,

For Leigh Alan,

Forever . . .

". . . the Noise and the Astonishment of the People at seeing me rise and walk, was not to be expressed."

—Jonathan Swift, *Gulliver's Travels*

"Manute Bol is so skinny they save money on road trips. They just fax him from city to city."

—**Woody Allen**

Contents

FOREWORD

The figure stands on a hill and looks across the African land-scape. The sun is round and bright and red behind him. The figure is in silhouette. Who is he? Hard to tell. His body is tall, tall, very tall. Slender. Thin. He could be a Giacometti sculpture. He could be Gumby. He could be the tallest, thinnest man there ever was. He suddenly turns. He begins to walk. He walks with a purpose, taking long strides, unbelievably long strides. Tall. Very tall.

A giraffe, eating leaves from the top of a tree, stops and no-tices. Who can this be? The figure walks. A hippopotamus, deep in the mud, notices. His large eyes follow the figure's progress. The figure walks. A group of children playing children's games notice. They have never seen anyone so tall, yet they are not afraid. They smile and giggle. The figure walks.

He walks across all the land he has known as a youth, walks through the pastures where he has taken care of the cows, walks through the highlands and walks through the swamp, through the day and the night. He walks farther than he has ever walked, past all the places he has been as a young man. He walks across bridges and through fields and forests. He walks and walks. He walks beyond the farthest known boundaries. He walks through the heat. He walks through sudden rain. He walks straight ahead, from one world to another.

Who is he?

"And at center. . . ."

So tall.

"Number eleven . . ."

So very tall.

"Man-uuuuuuuuute . . ."

Who?

"*Bol.*"

The figure suddenly stands in the center of a polished wooden floor inside a large arena. A spotlight is focused on his black face. The rest of the arena is dark, except for bubbles of light that spin and dance across the outlines of thousands of people. Music is playing, amplified so loud it hurts your ears. There is cheering, louder and louder, a noise as loud as the music. *Ma-nute. Ma-nute. Ma-nute.* How many people? Who knows? The figure stands with his shoulders back. Proud. A purple mascot, with the word *HOOPS* written across the front of his shirt, comes up to the figure and puts his right hand high. The figure answers, putting his right hand high. He slaps it against the mascot's purple fur hand. The crowd cheers even louder.

This is a fable.

This is the truth.

I follow the figure's steps, notebook in hand. The tall man. The taller-than-tall man. His shoe size is 15½. I write that down. I am captured by the sight of him, drawn along by a sense of wonder. I want to know where he has been and where he is going and what he is going to do next. I have never seen anyone like him.

"What are you working on?" friends ask.

"I am doing a book on Manute Bol."

"Manute Bol? Why would anyone do a book on Manute Bol? He never scores. He never plays. He never . . ."

I find I always have to explain. I start talking about Africa and cows and civil war. I talk about Division II college basketball and minor-league basketball and parts of basketball that never make the newspapers. I talk about scams and dreams and about learning the English language from the first word as an adult. Is not the good story supposed to be based on a journey, a quest? I talk about the longest journey, the largest quest I have ever seen, undertaken by the longest, largest person I have ever seen.

"Manute Bol is Rocky Balboa," I say. "Only better."

"Rocky Balboa?"

"Manute Bol is the Peter Sellers character, Chance the Gardener, in the movie *Being There*. Remember Chance the Gardener, the guy who was let loose in a society he did not understand yet somehow understood it better than anyone else?"

"Chance the Gardener."

"Manute Bol is the Eddie Murphy character from *Coming to America*. African royalty. He is the native from *The Gods Must Be Crazy*, except he is holding a basketball instead of a Coke bottle. He is . . ."

I have never wanted to do one of those well-made sports books, those as-told-to biographies of some superstar billionaire, following his cookie-cutter career from championship to championship, success to success, Little League to the pros. Who cares? I work instead on the tale of this seven-foot-seven expatriate from the jungles of the Sudan who now sits on the end of a bench in the National Basketball Association and makes $1.5 million per year and addresses Congress and trades jokes with David Letterman and Arsenio Hall.

"I am rewriting *My Fair Lady*," I finally explain.

"Yes?"

"In my version, Eliza Doolittle has been transformed into a seven-foot-seven black man. With tribal scars on his head."

I fly to Khartoum sitting next to a man in a turban who spits eight times into his little discomfort bag during the three-hour final leg of the trip. I count the number of spits. I write that down. I go to my room in a hotel that has armed guards at the front door searching women's purses. I look out the window at midnight, one hour after curfew in this country under martial law. I see packs of wild dogs running across the dirt street. I write that down.

I watch basketball in Cairo. I stand next to the team from the Ivory Coast as the players sing a tribal chant for inspiration. I talk with a basketball player from Senegal who went to school at the University of Maine. He says he was cold all the time. I write that down. I see a forward from Egypt in his uniform, on his knees, praying on a concrete corridor floor in the direction of Mecca. I ride a camel behind the players from Cameroon, heading toward the pyramids.

I sit in a bar in Cleveland with the Philadelphia 76ers—not a good team on the court, but filled with an old-time rowdiness off it. The tag end of a wedding reception is also in the bar. The bride and groom ask Charles Barkley, the Sixers star, to autograph a champagne bottle. He does better. Married? He orders another bottle of champagne for the wedding party table. The best man comes to Barkley. He says this is the groom's third marriage, the bride's second. Barkley wonders if he can get the champagne back.

I talk with a woman in Boston who works for Oxfam America, an organization trying to feed starving people in Africa. She says she has made many trips to that continent and says that the food is not very good for the relief visitors either. She describes a special occasion when a chicken was killed for dinner. The chicken was one tough bird. The woman found that she could not chew through the meat. It was sort of stuck on her teeth. One of the natives, who had attended college in the United States, saw her predicament. "What do you think?" he said. "Isn't this finnnnger-lickin' good?" I write that down.

I am in a drug clinic in Houston when Roy Tarpley, a former Dallas Mavericks star, appears with the news that he has passed his latest drug test. Congratulations are extended by everyone in the office. I do not know him, but I extend my congratulations, too. I go home. Two days later, I read that he has been arrested for punching a woman in a parking lot.

I try to pursue an old rumor with a former college coach. The rumor is that inmates at a prison were writing term papers for the players on the former coach's team. He asks who told me this. I honestly say I don't remember. It was a long time ago. He laughs. He changes the subject. Much later in the conversation he is being evasive about something else. He laughs again. He says he has to save some material for himself. He is thinking about writing his own book. He says that I may find out about those term papers then.

I renew acquaintance with a man who started a basketball league. He was friendly with my brother-in-law and offered him a franchise. My brother-in-law thought about it. He's an accountant. He is also a basketball fan. I told him at the time that I didn't know much about much, but I did not think a minor-league basketball franchise was exactly a blue-chip stock. He ultimately did not buy. The man says now that the league killed everyone who invested that first season.

I go to Bridgeport, Connecticut, and Newport, Rhode Island, and Oakland, California. I hear Chuck Daly, the coach, say that he knew his Detroit Pistons were truly world champions when he came to practice the next fall and every veteran in the room was making a call on a personal cellular phone. I write that down. I sit in a little Arabian coffee shop where most of the patrons seem to be smoking from those glass-bubbler hookahs. I order a Pepsi. I listen to a social worker from Washington about the problems of the Third World, about the fact that nobody cares, that nobody listens, that the Sudan and Somalia and Mozambique and Haiti and so many places with people of color have simply been forgotten. What can I do? I nod my head in agreement. I write that down, too.

I talk with people about basketball and politics and handbags and phonetics and milk. Any subject seems to count. I talk about beer and religion and driving a car and going to Disney World and watching movies and traveling on buses and singing songs and getting married and getting divorced. I talk about height: unbelievable, extraordinary height, height that can make a simple game seem easy, height that can send men scurrying across continents with greedy, Humphrey Bogart eyes, height that can take one man and dip him in gold, make him an object of desire.

Manute. I talk with people about Manute.

I am white.
Manute is black.
I am middle aged.
Manute is, well, probably not yet middle aged.
I am short, five feet nine inches.
Manute is certainly tall.

I have grown up in America with American food and American ideas and a certain American complacency about how life should be.

Manute has grown up as far away from all of that as could ever be imagined.

I have played basketball for most of my life. I still play basketball, a squat old-timer, tossing up jump shots at my local YMCA. I have never touched the rim, except while standing on a stepladder. I have never been paid a cent for playing basketball.

Manute has learned basketball in almost a Berlitz crash course. He can touch the rim without leaving his feet. He plays in the most exclusive professional league in all of sport, a league of millionaire athletes. He is a millionaire.

I am a creature from the normal, charted land.

Manute is from the stars.

I follow. I go to the assorted places where hope was spread out like so many bread crumbs leading to a gingerbread house containing a shiny floor and glass backboards and luxury boxes and fame and wealth. I climb the beanstalk at the end and talk to my subject.

"I never heard of America until 1979," he says.

What?

"I never heard of America until 1979," he repeats. "I never heard of basketball until 1979."

This is a fable.

This is the truth.

Once upon a time, a giant appeared in our midst . . .

No, not once upon at time.

Now.

Maybe as recently as today.

Noon time. At lunch.

Manute Bol walks through the front door of the TGI Friday's restaurant on Center Line Avenue at the edge of Philadelphia, and of course he has to duck. He is seven feet seven inches tall. The door has not been built for a man this size. Seven feet seven inches. Not much really has been built for a man this size. His head is caught in an obstacle course of doorways and lighting fixtures and ceiling fans that churn like so many airplane propellers on an upside-down runway. He does not seem to notice. This is the way it always is. No big deal.

A bunch of young people sit in the foyer, huddled on benches, filling out applications for employment. The writing stops. *Who the . . . What the . . .* He is almost a comic-strip character come to life. His face is sports-page famous. His size is everyplace overpowering. He is a shock to the eyes, whether they recognize exactly who he is or not. Manute Bol. Here.

"Hey, Nute, my man . . ."

"Manute . . . "

"Does he play basketball?"

The buzz is nothing new. The buzz is everywhere he goes. The most famous movie stars can put on false beards and strange hats and maybe a pair of sunglasses and wander the streets in anonymity. Manute Bol always has to be himself in public. A funny hat would do nothing except make him taller.

He acknowledges his name with a nod, then another, but really looks at no one. Duck. Duck again. The hostess automatically greets him and tells him his special table is ready. A second buzz, the same buzz, follows as he walks through the restaurant. New eyes see the same sight. How can a man be so big? How can he live like that? What problems must he have? Is he married? Jesus, Martha. He is thinner than thin, darker than dark. He looks like a giant version of those bendable figures that you might hang from a rearview mirror or from the handle on the door of the family refrigerator. His blackness is as overpowering as his height, a pure, concentrated black, a moonless midnight, the ultimate black chip on any color chart. Could anyone ever be taller? Could anyone ever be blacker? Jesus, Martha.

His table is in the back, near the bar. He eats here often, the restaurant close to St. Joseph's College, where the Philadelphia 76ers practice when they are home. The table is high, almost five feet off the ground. A normal person would climb onto the tall accompanying bar stool and sit with his feet on one of the two rungs. Manute sits and spreads his feet wide on the floor. Most of his height is in his legs. The inseam on the pants to his warm-up suit is 48 inches. His legs are taller than some people. He is wearing a black leather jacket with the letters NBA on the back and his name, Bol, stitched across the left breast in white letters. It is an expensive jacket, street-gang fashionable, part of the hip-hop now, but on Manute it is mute, quiet. What clothes can compete with the picture he presents?

"Heineken, Manute?" the waitress asks.

"Heineken," he says.

He has driven here in his van, a Winnebago, the sort of van hotels use to shuttle passengers to and from the local airport. A trail of rap music has been left in its wake, the bass lines floating in the air. He is married. Yes, he is married. He has three children, two boys and a girl. His custom-built house is in a Washington, D.C., suburb, but he has rented a condo in New Jersey for the season. He also owns a house in Alameda, California, another in Alexandria, Egypt, and two more in Khartoum in the Sudan. His age is a matter of debate, no records kept of his birth, but he is probably somewhere between twenty-eight and thirty-five. He says he is twenty-eight. He is in his seventh year of professional basketball, now with his third team in the National Basketball Association. His salary, guaranteed, is $1.5 million for the season. It is not an extravagant salary, perhaps, in the game he plays, where salaries can run as high as $6 million per year. It is extravagant everywhere else. He is borderline rich, at least.

The records show that he is the tallest man ever to play in the NBA, a league that has always put a great premium on height. Thirty or forty years ago, if he somehow had reached the United States, he might have traveled the country with a sideshow, standing in a tent in a field outside, say, Indianapolis, customers paying to look at him next to a woman with a beard or a two-headed goat. But this is a different time. The money is in basketball. He is not a great player, not even very good, as a matter of fact. He is tall. He can stand in the big arenas of the land and stretch his arms high and they are at the level of the ten-foot basket. He is a human impediment, a thin pine tree planted in front of the basket. He can wave his branches and create situations that other players mostly have not seen. This is worth the $1.5 million per year.

"Are you ready to order?" the waitress asks.

"I will have the steak," he says.

The menu describes his order as the "Friday's Classic—New York Strip. USDA choice aged beef, hand cut and charbroiled to perfection. $12.95." He does not look at the menu. His left hand is curled around the Heineken bottle, the bottle looking very small. His right hand is on the table, three of the long, blacker-than-black fingers curled at the end, the result of a hereditary birth defect. His teammates sometimes say he has "E.T. fingers." The menu sits. Even if he looked at it he would simply order "the steak" or "the chicken" or some other dish. The particulars and the sales pitch are of no interest. He mostly cannot read.

"Miss?" he says.

"Yes?"

"I also will have a glass of Korbel champagne. With the meal."

He talks about Africa. He talks about the bush, the swamp in the lower half of the Sudan, where he was born and raised. He talks about the morning practice. He talks about the traffic in the center of the city, about the weather, about tribal rituals. There is a wonderful, disjointed sense of here and there. An unreality.

The television at the bar is tuned to CNN Headline News, electronic beams shot from around the world and somehow brought together on this twenty-three-inch screen in this noisy restaurant. He talks about a place where the electronic beams never landed, a place where houses were made of mud and where giraffes would visit to snack on the grass-covered roofs, a place of *National Geographic* innocence. This is a dating bar at night, for goodness' sake, but what do these people know about dating? His grandfather was a tribal chief, supposedly seven feet ten inches tall with forty wives and more than eighty children. His mother was the second of his father's seven wives. That's dating. He sips his champagne. He talks.

"I had this girlfriend, she lived seven miles, eight miles away from my village," he says. "I would walk to her house every night. It was very scary, you know, because you have those lions out there. We grow a lot of corn. The lions would be inside the corn fields. Very scary. I would go with this flashlight. Seven miles. I have a club, like a baseball bat. I have a lot of spears on my back, maybe eleven spears. You need those for the lions. The lions are afraid of the flashlight. You need it. We have a saying, 'God saves people.' I think it is true. Because we have a lot of snakes out there, too. The king cobra. A lot of snakes. I would be walking through the night. I don't know how I did it, man. I don't think I could do it now. Seven miles, see the girl . . . and you couldn't stay in her house if you weren't married. I'd have to walk the seven miles back, too."

A civil war is roaring through his country now. His Dinka tribesmen are in the middle, fighting on the wrong side of the Muslim government, troubled by disease and drought and starvation as well as the government forces and their allies. His village, Turalie, no longer exists. The dwellings have been destroyed. The people have scattered. Many have died. He grew up in a window of time after one civil war had ended and before this one began. He was allowed to live the old life. His land was the land of flora and fauna, of peril and pestilence, that Americans can only glimpse through the iron bars of a zoo. A child's picture-book life. A jungle book.

"The giraffes were beautiful, man," he says. "They come right into the yard. We love the giraffes. I remember, my father told me that we Dinka are tall because we love the giraffes. The giraffes love us, too. All kinds of animals out there. Alligators. Hippos. You better watch out for the hippos, man. They kill people."

Hippos.

"I would take care of the cows," he says. "I would sleep with them in the field. The cows were very important. You probably would not understand how we feel about the cows. They all have names, the cows. Everybody knows everybody else's cows. Just by sight. Say I lost one of my cows. I would go looking for her. I would meet you and you would say, 'Oh, I saw her over at this place.' You would remember. You would know my cows. We have men, they come and write a song for your cows. You pay them money. This is a special song for each of your cows. You sing the song to the cows."

Cows.

"The mosquitoes were very bad in the summer," he says. "The tsetse flies. All kinds of mosquitoes. My father died of malaria. He was in the bush. There was no medicine. I had malaria, but not bad. I was in Khartoum when I had it. I went to hospital."

Malaria.

His voice is soft, but the words often arrive in a hurry. A malapropism here and there, a mangled verb tense, indicate that English is a second language, but he has no obvious accent. His first language was Dinka, the language of his tribe, a totally oral language. His second language was Arabic. His foundation in English comes from American television. He still says, things like "So-and-so, come on down!" or "Wheel . . . of . . . Fortune," lines from quiz shows or situation comedies. He has picked up a touch of black American, playing in the NBA, but he says the words with a different cadence. Like an announcer from the BBC trying to rap with kids on a ghetto street corner in Watts, he knows the words, but they do not sound right. He is not afraid to sprinkle a fine paprika of curse words into his conversation, but he does not sprinkle much now. He is talking about Africa.

"We would not eat much meat," he says. "We eat grains a lot. We eat corn. Sudanese dishes. We drink a lot of milk. I remember, I came here, the food all seemed so dry. I could not eat it for the longest time. I like chicken now. I like steak. I can eat a hamburger. I wish I could get some good milk. What is this pasteurized milk, this low-fat milk? The cow does not give pasteurized milk, low-fat milk. You drink the wrong milk here. I wish I had my own land, my own cows. I saw George Foreman, the boxer, on television the other night with his land and his cows. I would like my own cows."

He describes a Dinka ritual for adolescent boys called the *toc*. For a designated time, maybe as long as seven months, the adolescent boy's only duty is to drink milk. He is given a designated number of cows, maybe as many as ten, and he drinks all of their milk every day. Manute says he had to do this twice. He would drink and sit, drink and sit. Other boys were doing the same thing. There was a contest. On a designated day, the people of the tribe would gather and vote for the boy they thought had become the fattest. It was a beauty contest for fat. The winner would receive no prize except the applause.

"You drink the milk . . . I was really no good at it," Manute says. "I would say, 'This is bullshit.' But I did it. I would drink more than twenty gallons of milk a day. You drink that much milk, you can just feel it moving around inside you. You can't do nothing. You can't even move. You just sit under a tree, because that much milk, you just turn your head, the milk starts to become sour. You know that taste? You cannot move or the milk becomes sour.

"I got up to 250 pounds, I guess, but it is weight you lose very quickly. Especially in the summer because it is so hot. My cousin, he got so fat he could not walk. This is true. He weighed over six hundred pounds. His legs were so fat, so close together, he could not walk. If he had to walk from here to St. Joseph's, it would take him two days. That is how fat he was. Very fat."

The reminders of another adolescent ritual are on Manute's forehead. Four thin lines can be seen at each side. His blackness obscures the lines, almost makes them seem to be natural wrinkles, but if you look you can see them. These are Dinka tribal scars, cut into the skin when he was fourteen years old by a Master of the Fishing Spear. The process has become optional now in tribal society, but there were no options when he was young. He had run away from home for a while, run away from the thought of the scars, but in the end he succumbed. There were no options.

"You were considered a young boy unless you had the scars," he says. "You could not meet girls. It is a group thing, and who are you to be different? My father wanted me to get married because my mom had passed away. I came back. They cut you with a big knife, a sharp knife. You bleed a lot. You cannot cry. If you cry, they remember you forever as someone who cried. They make songs about you crying. Your family does not talk to you forever. You cannot cry. You sing songs while they are cutting, to show that you are not crying, songs about your family, your cows, maybe about how beautiful your father's wife is. You sing for fourteen, fifteen minutes. You do not cry."

A third ritual was the removal of six lower teeth. Most boys have their teeth removed when they are younger, at seven or eight, but Manute had the teeth removed one day, the scars cut on his face the next. Again, he could not cry. He considers the removal of the teeth a mistake.

"I should not have let them do it," he says. "But what are you going to do? They put these two sharp sticks—like toothpicks maybe, but much bigger—on either side of the tooth. They push it out. I did not want it done, but I did not cry. It's better now, you get a choice. When I had it done, there's maybe fifty other kids having it done, too."

There is little emotion as he talks. A smile for the giraffes, perhaps, a nervous laugh for the lions. Nothing, really, for the scars and teeth. He could be describing a boyhood in Steubenville, Ohio. This was natural. This was what happened. There were no cars, so everyone walked. There was no television. There were no books. There was no electricity. His life was the tribal life, insular and pure, the same life his ancestors and their ancestors had lived. The leading edge of civilization was not so far away, maybe three days by foot, but not many people wanted to walk up to it.

His father did not really work. There were a few crops and some cows, but his father did not do much work. The father was a local judge of sorts, the son of the famous tribal chief, so he sometimes settled disputes about cows or money or insults. The family had a piece of land, and there was food everywhere. Why should life change? Manute says his father's plan was for him to follow the same path: To raise some cows. To marry some women. To take care of his sister. To live the way everyone had always lived and would live forever.

"My father never wanted me to go to school," Manute says. "So I never went to school."

Never?

"Except for one year," he says. "At the University of Bridgeport."

The waitress collects the empty plates and glasses and brings the check. There is music in the background, Paula Abdul noise. This is lunch, so there are young men in suits in the restaurant, young women in business tweed. The other sounds mingle on the audio track: silverware on plates, conversation about office politics and personal relationships, laughter. The waitresses wear red-and-white-striped shirts and black pants. The look of a barber shop quartet. They have pins on their shirts, little slogans and logos. *Kiss me, I'm Italian.*

Manute stands. The buzz begins again.

A man asks him for his autograph. He says Manute is great and the Sixers are looking great and they had two great wins over the weekend. Manute signs a napkin. A woman asks him, shyly, if he is Manute Bol. She was wondering. He says he will check. Yes, he thinks he is Manute Bol. He signs a piece of paper for her. There are other people, on the fringe, who would like to say something, do something to have a moment of contact, but they are afraid. They stand. They stare. He walks past.

In the parking lot he says he thinks he'll take a drive to Washington in the Winnebago. He says he likes to do this once a week or so, simply to make sure the house is all right. The house is custom-built on the inside, eight-foot doors, tall ceilings, everything built for the oversized man, but on the outside it is quite normal. He wants a normal-looking house. Enough people stare at the owner without staring at the house.

As he starts to move toward the Winnebago, there is the sound of someone pounding on the restaurant window. Manute turns. The pounder is Charles Barkley, Manute's teammate and NBA All-Star, a subject of constant controversy. A wicked smile has crossed Barkley's face. He extends the middle finger of each hand and raises the fingers high in the window. He sticks out his tongue. Manute raises a middle finger in return.

"That C.B.," he says. "He's a crazy motherfucker."

The Winnebago awaits.

*The sight of the giant stirred the imaginations
of ordinary men. It seemed as if he must possess
extraordinary powers. Why, look at him.
Just look.
He was so tall that if he reached up . . .*

Just put up his hands . . .

He could probably touch . . .

The sky?

EIGHT

Jimmy Lynam was there at the beginning. Not the true beginning perhaps, not with the giraffes and the tsetse flies in Africa, not when Manute had never seen a basketball, but Jimmy Lynam was there for the American beginning. He learned the secret early, the secret that the tallest man anyone had ever seen had arrived in the country to play this game.

"Listen to this," Jimmy Lynam says. "I'm sitting in my office. The phone rings. A guy named Don Feeley, who coached at Fairleigh Dickinson, is on the line. I knew him a little bit because he once coached at Sacred Heart in Bridgeport, Connecticut, and I coached at Fairfield University, which was close. The NBA draft is five days away and he says he has a sleeper for me. I say, 'Yeah, yeah, a sleeper. Everybody has a sleeper.' They're always nice kids, work hard, can't play a bit. I've never seen a sleeper who was any good. Feeley tells me his sleeper is seven feet seven inches. I begin to listen."

Seven feet seven.

Height.

Is there any quality more attractive to any basketball man anywhere? Height is the fuel of the basketball dream. Height makes the game so much easier, the coach so much smarter. Height. The object of the game is to put a 9½-inch-diameter ball through an eighteen-inch-diameter iron ring that is suspended ten feet off the ground. Simple mathematics takes care of the rest. The closer a hand is to the basket, the better it can control the activity around the basket. Height.

What sins have not been committed in the search for the tall, taller, tallest basketball player imaginable? The game is a hundred years old and money has been put into strange hands, women have been brought to strange motel rooms, friendships have ended and reputations ruined, all to romance the kid who stands in the middle of the class picture, back row, head and shoulders above everyone else. School district boundaries have been redrawn. Famous institutions of higher learning have been placed on probation. Multimillion-dollar contracts have been signed. For height.

The year was 1983. Lynam was the new coach of the San Diego Clippers, a deadbeat franchise that was expected to finish at the bottom of the standings again. The shelf life of a coach in that situation is not very long. (Indeed, Lynam would be fired in the middle of his second season.) The hope has to be that something will happen fast, that some dramatic turnaround will occur. A surprise will appear during the draft, a couple of veterans will respond to a different sort of coaching stimulus, something. In short, a miracle will happen. The coach will be known forever as a basketball genius, the subject of assorted biographies, and the author of many textbooks.

The addition of great height, of course, would be a great miracle. The greatest.

"I had grown up in Philadelphia when Wilt Chamberlain was in high school here," Lynam says. "He's, what, five years older than me? He went to Overbrook High School. He used to play at the playground right across the street. We'd go there, the little kids. We'd sit around, mostly watch. If they needed an extra guy or two we'd play, but mostly we'd watch. I played with Chamberlain a few times, but mostly I just watched him. He was just God. He could do anything he wanted. Everyone else . . . he did whatever he wanted. I still say he was the greatest of them all."

Chamberlain was seven feet one, later to be celebrated as the most versatile big man of all time, playing in Philadelphia, San Francisco, and Los Angeles, dunking the ball and scowling for the camera, and apparently learning how to dance with pretty women at the same time. He was a doodle from a coach's notebook come to life, the biggest X imaginable to place against the five opposition Os on the blackboard. If a coach had a first choice to start a team, with all the players in the history of the game available, a lot of coaches would agree with Lynam: pick the big man in the middle, Chamberlain, first.

Now there was a man six inches taller? Here? Available? Maybe he couldn't play like Chamberlain. Who could? Maybe he couldn't play at all. Maybe he was totally uncoordinated, anemic, knock-kneed, and slower than a snail crossing a supermarket parking lot on a hot afternoon. No matter; if he could breathe, he was worth a look.

"So Feeley says the guy is in Cleveland now," Lynam says. "He's going to go to Case Western Reserve to take some English classes, doesn't know a word of English, and the coach at Cleveland State is going to try to get him into school. Feeley is wondering if maybe the guy can skip all that and come straight to the pros. The guy is wondering, too. I ask Feeley if he's told anyone else about this. Feeley says he called Frank Layden, the coach of the Utah Jazz, but Layden said he already had Mark Eaton at seven feet four and felt he couldn't really bring another unknown big player to camp. People would think he was running some kind of circus. Feeley says I'm the second one he called. I tell him, 'Don't call anyone else.' "

The search for the big man in basketball is so basic that it sometimes seems to be one of the game's rules. Two points for a basket. One point for a free throw. Pick the big man. Stand around any playground or in any YMCA gymnasium in any part of America, any part of the world, and watch the start of a pickup game. Two captains are chosen. Fingers are thrown, odds against evens. One captain wins the right to make the first pick from the available talent. Who does he choose? Nine times out of ten the selection is made with a yardstick. Size counts. Size counts a lot. *I'll take Stretch.*

"Height just implies so much in basketball," says Pete Newell, former University of California coach and a longtime authority on big men. "When you put a big man in the middle of your lineup, you not only have offensive control, because he is so close to the basket, but you have certain protections on defense. There are so many connotations on defense to a big man—he guards against the lay-up and the short jump shot, he controls the rebounds, he starts your team back down the floor on offense. He changes everything for the other team. Other players on the floor . . . no one can have the control of the big man. The greatest point guard you can find might be wonderful offensively, but he isn't going to give you that defensive control that a big man will. No one else will."

The history of the game is almost the history of big men, the names of its dynasties usually tied to the names of centers, especially in the pros. From the dominance of the Minneapolis Lakers and six-foot-ten George Mikan, to the Boston Celtics teams of six-foot-nine Bill Russell, to the Los Angeles Lakers teams of seven-foot-two Kareem Abdul-Jabbar, the big man has been a foundation. Chamberlain at seven feet one made all of his teams instant contenders. Seven-foot Bill Walton would still be winning championships with the Portland Trailblazers if he had stayed healthy. The college teams of all of these players were powerhouses—the UCLA dynasties of Walton and Abdul-Jabbar, the winning streak of Russell at the University of San Francisco—and, no doubt, their high school teams were as well. The old coach's line, probably said first by James Naismith when he attached that first peach basket to that gymnasium wall in Springfield, Massachusetts, is that "you can't teach height." You either have it or you don't.

"I had Walton at Portland," Dr. Jack Ramsey, a Hall of Fame coach, says. "You're just blessed when you have a big man. I had him for that championship season, then he broke his foot the next season and was never the same. That one season . . . the game was so much easier. He rebounded, he scored, he took care of the defensive end. And he passed. He was such a good passer. He opened up so many opportunities for everybody else. I don't think anyone could ever do as many things as he could. But his body just wasn't built to stand up to the pounding."

There have been attempts to limit the big man's efficiency, changes in rules to stop him from simply squashing a missed shot into the basket at every opportunity (goaltending) or flicking it away from the rim (also goaltending), changes in rules that have made him stand away from the backboard for much of the time (three seconds violation in the foul lane). There have been debates about lowering the basket or making it higher. Nothing has really worked. The big man has simply kept pace, dominating. As the game has become bigger, the big men have become faster, more coordinated, and, well, bigger.

"You look at the champions of our league," Lynam says. "On most of them, you could find that a big man was a major factor. I suppose Detroit, the Detroit Pistons, did it without a big man, but even they didn't win everything until they found a big man in James Edwards. The Chicago Bulls, I suppose, with Michael Jordan . . . but Bill Cartwright was a piece they needed. You need a big man somewhere. The big man is the place to start."

Even the case of Jordan, the Bulls' star, generally regarded now as the best all-around player in the history of the game, illustrates the mania for big men. Where was Jordan picked in the 1984 NBA draft? Third. The first pick that year was Hakeem Olajuwon from Houston. Big man. The second pick was Sam Bowie from Kentucky. Big man. Third pick? The best all-around player in the history of the game was "only" six feet five. Height sometimes seems to mean everything.

"To tell the truth, I got four kids and unfortunately only one is playing ball," Jordan's father, James, says. "Larry . . . the brother who is one year older than Michael, he taught Michael everything he knows. But Larry's only about five feet nine."

"I was six feet seven when I went to college, but I grew two inches when I was there," Boston Celtics forward Larry Bird says, describing the importance of height. "If I hadn't grown those two inches, I might not have been able to play in the NBA. Simple as that. And if I did play, it would all have been different. I couldn't have been the player that I have been."

The search for the big man, for the ultimate height, generally begins early in America, the prospect spotted in the first year of high school, if not earlier. What is the traditional story? Basketball coach is walking across parking lot to high school office. Coach sees high school band practicing Sousa marches on the football field. Coach notices strange irregularity in formation. Is that a tall kid in the trumpet section? Coach sends message to kid. Kid comes to office. Coach offers team jersey. Ten years later, kid is driving five expensive cars and endorsing after-shave lotions and signing his autograph only for money. An American dream. Kids are not stupid. They follow where their bodies lead them.

"I liked to play baseball," says seven-foot-four Ralph Sampson, former college player of the year and former Houston

Rocket. "I still like to play baseball. The taller I got, though, the larger my strike zone got. I moved to basketball."

"I played hockey," says Kevin McHale, six-foot-ten forward for the Celtics. "I just kept growing. It was ridiculous to keep playing hockey."

"I grew six and a half inches in three months," says Bill Walton. "I was fourteen years old, recovering from knee surgery. All I did for three months was lie down and eat. I thought I was going to become heavy. I came out of the cast and I had gained seven pounds and six and a half inches. I remember my parents were really mad that I had no clothes that fit, even though I was still as skinny as you could imagine. Just this big, skinny kid."

The cultivation of the big, skinny kid can be relentless. He is sent to special summer camps. He is given nutritional programs to follow. He is placed on special traveling all-star teams to play in special tournaments. He is a celebrity by the end of his sophomore year in high school, treated with respect by famous coaches whose names he's read in the newspapers. Where will he go to college? What will he do? Even if he is not a very good basketball player yet, he is considered a resource that can be developed. Height, alone, makes him special.

"It's amazing how much these college coaches think about height," a Boston AAU coach, Ron Miglioccia, says. "I have a team. . . . the best sixteen-year-old kids from the area. Some very, very good basketball players. Forwards. Guards. Not too tall, but great players. As a favor, I add this seven-foot kid from the western part of the state. He's not much of a player at all, shouldn't be on the team, but I add him. The college coaches come to practice. Who do they all ask about? The big kid. He's the only kid they want to know. He can't play . . . they say they'll teach him. I don't know. The kid had trouble catching the ball. He just couldn't reach it or something. My point guard asks me what to do. I say, 'From now on, just throw all your passes at the kid's face. That way he has to get his hands up to catch the ball.'

We go onto the court. The point guard throws the pass, right at the kid's face . . . breaks the kid's nose. There you are. The only kid the coaches want to see."

Where does he live? How well does he play? What does he want? The big kid is the odd difference. The normal-size kid comes off a conveyor belt, point guards and power forwards arriving on the scene in enough quantities to satisfy general demand. The big kid? The big man? He is a character touched by the finger of a smiling basketball deity. In the rest of life the kid may be seen as a clumsy, out-sized figure, a freak, an oddity, someone to be almost pitied as he contends with a world built for the Lilliputians instead of Gulliver. In basketball? The rules change.

Patrick Ewing, now the All-Star center for the New York Knicks, seven feet one, was being recruited in high school. A college assistant coach took him to a restaurant at the Cambridge Hyatt Hotel. The restaurant was on the top floor with a skyline view of Boston. Ewing was ill at ease. He was wearing the clothes of a high school senior and everyone else seemed to be wearing expensive suits. The college assistant was wearing an expensive suit.

"What's the matter?" the assistant asked Ewing.

"All these people seem so rich," Ewing said.

"Patrick," the assistant said with a smile. "You're richer than any of them. Your money is just being held in escrow."

"Listen to this," Lynam says. "I decide to draft the guy. Manute. I've never seen him. I've never seen a picture. I decide to draft him. A late round. I figure it's worth a shot."

Lynam, fifty, tells his story with a Philadelphia street-corner excitement. *Listen to this.* He touches the listener's arm when he talks. He is a short man, a former point guard at St. Joseph's, good dribbler, no shooter. He still has longish hair, a fifties cut with a hint of a drop curl ready to fall. When he stands in front of a bench, wearing a double-breasted suit and Italian shoes, his team seated behind him, he sometimes looks like the leader of a doo-wop chorus on some oldies revival tour. *Listen to this.* He talks as if he is remembering the time he saw Babe the Blue Ox walk down Broad Street, or the time he had a tip on a horse that should have paid off, should have made everyone millions.

On draft day, when the available talent was chosen by the NBA, Lynam was in San Diego. At the other end of a phone, Howard Garfinkel was submitting the Clippers' choices at the draft headquarters in New York. Garfinkel is known as a supreme basketball talent evaluator. He runs the noted five-star camps in Pennsylvania and Virginia, which attract the best high school talent in the country every summer. He knows the names of all the good basketball players in the United States when they're thirteen years old. He knows heights, weights, shoe sizes, family situations. He knows everything. Lynam read off the Clippers' pick for the fifth round.

"Manute," Lynam said. "That's M-a-n-u-t-e."

"What's his first name?" Garfinkel asked.

"That is his first name. His second name is Bol. That's B-o-l."

"Never heard of him. Where's he from?"

"Sudan."

"Never heard of it. What kind of school is that?"

"It's not a school. It's a country."

"Never heard of it."

Wasn't this beautiful? Lynam was watching the proceedings on television on ESPN. The fifth round of the draft was usually boring, the players not really projected to make the team, everyone moving through a ritual dance. This was the time when eager kids from local colleges were drafted simply to make local headlines, or when too-short forwards and too-slow guards were picked to fill out training camp rosters. Someone from the NBA read off the name and the country and then the height and weight: seven feet seven inches, 180 pounds. What was this? A joke? There was a murmur of confusion around the draft tables.

NBA talent scout Marty Blake, another man who knows everything about everything, was questioned on the screen. Blake said he had never heard of any Manute Bol. Lynam laughed. The sleeper of sleepers. He still had not seen Manute in person.

"I went out to Cleveland a couple of weeks later to look at him," Lynam says. "He was playing in this pickup game against Darren Tillis, a six-foot-eleven guy the Celtics once took in the first round of the draft. I didn't know what to say. I'd never seen anyone like him. He needed a lot of work, but he was playing against a big kid who was a former first-round draft choice of the Boston Celtics and he was doing all right . . . and he was tall. Very tall. Listen to this, though. I go up to him after the practice and introduce myself. Manute has no teeth. He's got this other guy from the Sudan with him, Deng. Deng knows English, so he's doing all the translating. He and Manute are talking in this language I've never heard. I ask Deng what it is. He says, I think, 'Swahili.' "

Actually, the language was Dinka, but that didn't matter. Language, teeth, inexperience, nothing really mattered. Nothing except height. Lynam was not sure this big African guy in front of him could play against, say, Kareem Abdul-Jabbar, but he surely wouldn't have minded taking a training-camp look. Fifth round. The steal of steals? Already his mind was diagramming weird offenses and defenses on a blackboard, a mammoth X suddenly added to the other four Xs on the floor against the visiting five Os. Manute Bol, huh? He wanted to test the new possibilities. He was ready to offer a contract.

The rest of the story was not so free or easy. The contract was never signed. The NBA declared Manute ineligible on a technicality—he had not stated his intention to enter the draft forty-five days before it was held. He supposedly was under twenty-one. He supposedly was too young simply to walk into the NBA without declaring his intentions. Something like that. The draft selection was voided.

"Here's the thing," Lynam says. "Manute really should have

been with the Clippers. That was a legal pick. They should have kept his draft rights. Listen to this, the problem was supposed to be that he was too young for the draft, that was why he had to declare. Too young? It all got very confusing. One of the things the NBA was looking at was his passport. His passport said he was nineteen years old. Well, his passport also said he was five feet two."

Lynam asked Manute about the discrepancy. Manute said he had been sitting down when the Sudanese officials measured him.

The NBA had no experience with this kind of pick. No foreign player had ever played in the league. The slow addition of foreigners would begin in another year with the selection of big man Olajuwon of Nigeria and the University of Houston, but this was uncharted ground in 1983. Seven feet seven? From the Sudan? The search for talent traditionally had been an American search. The game was an American game, invented here, developed here, played at the highest level here. Why bother looking anywhere else? Who was there?

The exceptional money available in pro basketball is a recent development. Basketball stars are now paid like famous entertainers or the heads of multinational corporations. There was no great financial incentive for a foreign player to come here until this change. Why should he endure the hardships of a new country, new language, new customs, when he could be paid almost as well at home? American basketball, basically, was American basketball. A photo essay on tall Watusi tribesmen might set a few inventive minds wandering, but the wandering never translated into physical action. America thought of itself as the Mother Church of basketball, sending missionaries out to preach the virtue of the fifteen-foot, pull-up jump shot, not seeking talent to bring home. The few foreigners who did play in the

United States were curious visitors, looking for a free college education.

"I was drafted by the Atlanta Hawks, but I could make more money by going home to play in Europe," says Kresmir Cosic of Yugoslavia, possibly the first European to play Division I basketball when he went to Brigham Young University between 1969 and 1973. "If it happened now—the money now—I would have stayed, for sure, but then it wasn't any big thing. I did better by going home, playing for my country on the national team."

Cosic was seen mostly as a free-spirited aberration. He showed up in Provo, Utah, a big man at six feet ten, not knowing English, and rolled through his four years. He threw up wild hook shots, cursed at referees in Serbo-Croatian, laughed a lot, and was a very good player. Could there be another one out there like him? How could there? When asked if he was nervous about leaving home, he said, "I come from Zadar, a port on the Mediterranean. In my town, a man tells his wife he is going out for a pack of matches and comes back twenty years later from Argentina with a new wife and five kids. We are people who travel."

"Do you know what I remember from the United States?" Cosic says back in Zadar, his home in Croatia. "I went to the camp of the Boston Celtics one summer. Red Auerbach was the coach. All my life I have wanted to dribble the ball. All my life coaches have told me that I am a big man and big men do not dribble. One day, at the camp, I was covered and I threw a bad pass. Red Auerbach asked me why I didn't simply dribble away from the trouble. I told him all my coaches had told me that I should never dribble. He said, 'You're a good dribbler, you should dribble.' I have always thought he was the only coach I ever had who made decisions for himself. He saw with his eyes."

Newell, the big-man authority in California, was one of the few Americans who saw the possibilities of foreign players coming to play for American colleges and, perhaps, even the pros. As the game was played in more and more places, as the money grew, he saw more and more foreign big men. Why couldn't a foreign big man play here? Newell had worked with all sorts of big men, clumsy men, men who had to be taught the game as if it were an Arthur Murray course in ballroom dancing. Step. Step. Turn. Shoot. Couldn't the big man from another country also be taught? There seemed to be a lot of them out there.

"You look around the world, at the places where the big people come from," he says. "South America. Africa. That certain area of Yugoslavia along the coast. China . . . up north, the Mongolians. The biggest man I ever saw was from Japan. Chibi Okayama. Seven feet nine. He had some disease; he couldn't stop growing. It's usually a fatal disease. I think a big man in China, Mr. Mu, died of it. Well, Chibi—that's 'Tiny' in Japanese—came here. We had him fixed up to play at the University of Portland. He just couldn't do it. He was still growing, about three-quarters of an inch a year. The doctors sent him home to be treated with drugs to arrest the growth. He was in bed for like two years. The drugs worked, but he really couldn't play afterward. All of his movements were very slow. It's ironic, he's coming back to the United States this year. He's going to have an internship as an assistant coach at Western Michigan. The coach, Bob Donewald, called and asked me how much basketball Chibi knew, how much he would be able to help. I told him I wasn't sure, but I did know one thing, Western Michigan is going to look very good when it walks through airports this year."

The best of the foreign big men was a Russian, seven-foot-three Arvidis Sabonis. He started coming to the United States in the seventies as a teenager playing with the national team. Newell saw in Sabonis what he had not seen in any of the Americans he had been watching. He saw the new Wilt. The size, the coordination, were the same. Better. The future could have been as good.

"He was the best young big man I ever saw," Newell says. "The closest to Wilt. Tall as he was, he had the physical symmetry of a six-foot-seven forward, the same kind of agility. His hands were so big that he could catch the ball with one hand all the time and hold off the other guy with the other hand. I've never seen anyone else like that. I saw him make a play, under the basket in Japan. He got a rebound and was falling out of bounds and he looked over his shoulder and saw a teammate heading for the other basket and he just sort of backhanded the ball ninety feet. The length of the court. Perfect. I still don't know how he did it. It was sort of like throwing a backhand discus. He could have been great, but I think the system just got to him over there. He could never leave. He could never improve. Then he developed bad knees and that was that. If he'd been able to come here at seventeen, it would have been something."

In 1983, though, there was still little movement. Olajuwon was an exception, coming from the city streets of Lagos to play at the University of Houston. A German, Detlef Schrempf, was playing at the University of Washington. Another German, Uwe Blab, was at Indiana. There was no real scouting or recruiting outside the country; what happened simply happened. The Third World seemed out of the question. If European players weren't playing in the United States, what chance did players from underdeveloped countries have? The daydream about landing a big player was mostly still set on some farm in Iowa or the playgrounds of some Eastern ghetto. The first African player didn't play in Division I until 1978. Africa? The people in a game increasingly dominated by African-Americans somehow did not think so much about the African part.

"I'd never thought about Africa," Tom Penders, coach at the University of Texas, says as he begins his own miracle story about the first African arrival. "I couldn't have been more surprised. I was just sitting in my office. A man called me up with a seven-foot basketball player."

Penders was at Columbia University in 1978. The player's name was Dud (pronounced "Dude") Tongal. He was from the Sudan, same as Manute. He was a Dinka, same as Manute. He had the tribal scars on his forehead. He was seven feet one. His age was undetermined. This was where the similarities ended. He spoke English fluently. He was educated. His uncle was part of the Sudanese mission at the United Nations in Manhattan. A group of Americans, including former NBA All-Star Tiny Archibald and CCNY coach Floyd Layne, had gone to Africa to conduct a clinic, spreading the basketball word. Layne had met Tongal and mentioned that if he ever came to the United States, there was a chance he could play basketball at CCNY. Tongal liked the idea, contacted his uncle, and landed in New York.

"So it's the middle of the basketball season," Penders says. "Dud and his uncle go to watch CCNY play, up at the old gym, right at 138th and Convent. CCNY's game is against us, Columbia. We have a good team, a very good team. We win the game by about forty points. A blowout. Dud tells his uncle that he thinks he would rather go to Columbia than to CCNY. Because we won.

"I don't know any of this has happened. I never saw him. I'm in the office the next day and Dud's uncle calls me. I thought it was a joke. Guy from the Sudan. The United Nations. Has a seven-foot-one nephew who wants to go to Columbia. Sure. The nephew has great grades, speaks English very well. Sure. Who is this? I had nothing to do, though, so I kept listening, waiting for the punch line. After a while—the uncle spoke with an accent and everything—I started paying attention. I started thinking that this might be real. I took out a pad. I started writing down the information."

By the start of the next school year, Penders had moved along to Fordham University. Dud went with him, even bringing along another player from the Sudan, a smaller Dinka named Edward Bona. Dud and Bona played four years at Fordham, took a full course load, graduated. Neither player was a great star, but both developed in the four years and started on a Division I team. Penders never did find out how old Tongal was, but figured him to be almost thirty at graduation. This was a running joke for the four years. How old was Dud?

"He'd never show us his passport, birth certificate, or anything," Penders says. "What he did show us one day was this photograph. There was a guy in a soldier's uniform, holding a basketball in one hand and touching the basket with his other hand. The guy's feet were on the ground. It was an amazing photograph. 'Who's that?' I asked. 'That's my cousin,' Dud said.''

Penders was interested, of course. How tall could this guy be? The interest fell apart when he learned the cousin did not know English and had never been to school in his life. There were no grades, no transcripts, no diplomas. Nothing. What could Penders do? This was Fordham. There was no money to be flying to the Sudan to look for basketball players.

"The way it was explained to me, the Sudan is one of those countries where your future is determined when you're real young," Penders says. "Some people are sent to school and become educated. Doctors and lawyers and teachers. Other people never go to school. They're going to be farmers or workers. Everything is established very early by the fathers. This guy was a farmer. No school. I just forgot about him."

Listen to this. The cousin's name was Manute.

"You say to yourself, 'seven feet seven,' " Jimmy Lynam says. "This guy can change a game just by standing there. That's all he has to do. Stand there. If he does something else . . . how many players can come into a game and just change the game? Just standing there. You have to be interested."

This is early in the 1991–92 season. November. In the background, on the St. Joseph's practice floor, no more than twenty feet away, Manute is playing a game of one-on-one against a Sixers reserve named Dave Hoppen. Hoppen is six feet eleven but looks like a child against Manute. Every shot Hoppen takes is thrown with an exaggerated arc. Who throws a basketball that high? Every shot Manute takes is either a little hook shot, going right, or a spin to the left and a two-handed dunk. When he scores, Manute hoots. Hoooo-eeee. Hoppen laughs.

Lynam is the coach. Three years after he took the job, he obtained Manute at last, trading the Sixers' first-round choice in the 1991 draft, a heavy price, to the Golden State Warriors. The trade was controversial and the results have been mixed after one season. The second season is off to a slow start. The Sixers are not winning. Manute is playing only in limited spurts. Lynam still is positive. The Sixers publicity office pumps out numbers to show Manute's effectiveness, about how opposing teams always shoot a worse percentage when he's on the floor, about how he blocks more shots per minute of playing time than anyone in the NBA. There are other stats, about his offensive ineffectiveness, about his average of less than 2 points a game, about the fact that he has never scored in double figures in a single game for the Sixers, but those can be changed. Can't they?

"Three baskets a game," Lynam says to a group of reporters around him. "He can do that, can't he? Maybe take six shots, seven. Make three. Make the other team have to play him. Open things up. Three baskets. Isn't that possible? He can do that."

Manute reaches over Hoppen. Manute dunks.

The picture is so deceiving. How much work has been done to reach this place, to score this one, simple basket? How many hours, days, years? How many obstacles have been overcome? The story stretches back past anything Lynam knows, back and back and back. Miles and years. A tribal drum sounds. The jungle animals watch. Manute bounces the ball and prepares for his next shot in the air-conditioned gym.

"Three baskets," Lynam says.

Seven feet seven.

Height is irresistible.

The giant came from a land that was far, far away. It was a place of many giants, but he was the biggest giant of them all. He lived a simple life in this place until one day someone handed him a round ball. What should he do with this round ball? That was the beginning.

Far, far away.

DINKAS

The different pieces of information on the front of the black sweatshirt are "Save the Planet," "Hard Rock Cafe," and "Orlando, Fla." The shirt, of course, came from Manute. Michael Malouk Wiet has never been close to a Hard Rock Cafe, much less Orlando, Florida. His place on the planet now is Cairo, Egypt. He sees America only in the abbreviated Cairo version, getting a daily dose in his job in the identification cards section of the American embassy. He comes off the crowded streets, with their low-lying smog and their gridlocked buses and their one-legged beggars and the perpetual pandemonium, into this armed American sanctuary that serves cheeseburgers and fries and devil dogs for lunch in the cafeteria.

"Hey, dude, where've you been?" a U.S. Marine in full fatigue battle dress, complete with automatic weapon slung over his shoulder, asks as Michael steps from the elevator on the seventh floor.

"Hello, little short man," Michael says.

"When are we going dancing?" the marine asks. "I want to go dancing. Take me to a place."

"I can't take you," Michael says. "Sorry, you don't have any rhythm."

This is the sort of joke Manute would use. Michael is Manute's cousin. There are many cousins, of course, with so many wives and so many children in a Dinka family tree, but he is twenty-nine years old, approximately the same age as Manute, and has been Manute's friend since they played basketball together in Khartoum. He has worked at the embassy for eight years. His English is good, learned at the missionary schools, bent into American dialect with his everyday American associations. Everyone in the embassy seems to know him. *Hey, Michael. Hey.* Everyone seems to smile when he passes.

"I've taken Manute here," Michael says. "I've taken him to meet the ambassador. Last summer I took him to the American University to play basketball. People came running from everywhere. The famous Manute Bol. The Dinka Man of the NBA. I'm the one who forced him to buy a house over here in Alexandria. I told him, 'Buy the house, come here, be near your people. See all the Dinka.' The war has sent so many people here. He bought the house in Alexandria, nice house, air-conditioning, beautiful. He keeps that for himself, locks it up when he is not here, but he also pays the rent for an apartment in Cairo where five families live. He pays the rent, whole year in advance. He is famous among our people. For America, I don't know how wealthy he is, but for Third World, for Africans, he is rich."

Michael has not been back to the Sudan since 1984 when he visited for eight weeks. He, like Manute, is an expatriate. The Arab government would make things hard for him if he returned. The customs officials would ask him why he had been away from his country for so long and why he had decided to return. He would be a suspicious character. He would probably wind up in jail. He has not seen his father and mother in the south of the Sudan in ten years. The last message he received from his country was smuggled to him, through Nairobi, Kenya, three months ago. The letter was from one of his brothers who is fighting on the side of John Garang, the Dinka rebel leader in the civil war.

"It is all so hard," Michael says. "Manute wants me to come to America, says he can get me a job, but I do not think so. My other brothers are here in Egypt. My people are here. I want to be close to my family, even if I cannot see them."

He has been married for a year. The traditional Dinka marital arrangement—a hundred cows to his wife's family for her father's consent—was amended. He will not have to pay the cows until the war is done. He says he is trying to make enough money to be married again. He says he will have three or four wives by the time he is finished. They will all live in the same house, along with all of their children. This is not unusual in this part of the world.

"The Muslims also have more than one wife, but they have to put each wife in a different apartment," Michael says. "We have them all in the same house. Night comes, you sleep with the one you want. The others become mad, but that is life. You sleep with them on other nights. This is the way we live. Manute will do this, too. He also has only one wife now, but I know he wants more. He wants ten, fifteen kids. My wife does not like the idea of another wife in the house, but I tell her that this is our Dinka culture. If she doesn't like it, I will not have her. That is how it is."

He drinks a Pepsi. He smokes a Winston cigarette. He is wearing jeans and Nike sneakers. An older man and his wife, both white, approach Michael in the cafeteria. The older man is smiling. He is from Detroit. He introduces his wife.

"Michael is Manute Bol's cousin," he says to his wife. "You remember Manute Bol. The basketball player?"

"Oh, yes, we saw him against the Pistons in Detroit," the woman says. "How is he doing?"

Michael Malouk Wiet says his cousin is doing fine.

*　　*　　*

A Dinka tribesman residing in the outside world is still an exotic surprise. Two and three generations ago, no more than four, he would have been in a foreign land only because his father or father's father had been captured and placed into slavery, probably by the Egyptians or Turks. The idea of leaving the south of the Sudan by free will, going someplace else to look for a better job, to live a better and modern life, would have been ridiculous. What could be a better life than to live with other Dinka people, to care for the cows, to tell stories long into the night, to live as Dinka had always lived? The Dinka consider themselves chosen people with a chosen way of life. Who would want to go somewhere far away? Ridiculous. Who would take the unknown over the lovely known?

One of the Dinka myths of creation, described by a chief named Loth Adija in *Africans of Two Worlds,* a book written by Dr. Francis Deng of the Brookings Institute in Washington, the first Dinka ever to gain a Ph.D., illustrates the situation.

"God asked man, 'which one shall I give you, black man; there is the cow and the thing called "What," ' " Adija says. "Which of the two would you like?"

"The man said, 'I do not want What.'

"Then God said, 'But What is better than the cow!'

"The man said, 'No.'

"God said, 'If you like the cow, you had better taste its milk first before you choose it finally.'

"The man squeezed some milk into his hand, tasted it, and said, 'Let us have the milk and never see What.' "

To leave friends and family—the term *family* extends to thousands of people in a tribe of over 2 million people—was an illogical choice. What "What" could possibly be so attractive?

The few incursions of outside society had been brutal and unpleasant. The Egyptians, the Turks, the Arab slave traders from the north—what could be gained from dealing with people who arrived with pistols and shot your men and took away your children? The Dinka phrase to describe the arrival of these various people was "the time the land was spoiled."

Only the British, arriving in force after the defeat and death of Gen. Charles ("Chinese") Gordon in Khartoum in 1885, and in loose control until 1955, seemed to offer any small positives. For the first time, an invader did not deal in slavery and, also for the first time, allowed local autonomy. The slave traders still came, but the British tried to stop them. The British seemed fair. Under the theory of "divide and rule," they allowed the Dinka to lead traditional lives with a traditional tribal structure of government, using the black Africans of the south to act as a balance to the lighter-skinned Muslims of the north. The one point the British did push was education. The missionaries arrived with Bibles and blackboards. Their advice was to learn English, to learn how to read, to learn about the rest of civilization.

The Dinka were skeptical. Why? Who needed to read? Who needed outside civilization? Civilization need only extend as far as a man could walk in a certain number of days. There was no need of these tales of great oceans and great men and machines and other nonsense.

"Going to school dates back no farther than the time of our grandfathers," Edward Bona, another of Manute's cousins, the player who followed Dud Tongal to Fordham, says. "Until then, the Dinka had lived the same traditional way for centuries, herding the cattle, living off the land. No change. The British wanted all the chiefs to send their people to school, to encourage education. The Dinka didn't trust the British. To live the traditional life, there was no need for school. What you had to learn—how to make rope, how to tie cattle down, how to find a pasture in a time of drought—were not things you would learn in a school.

A lot of Dinka, most Dinka, didn't believe school was necessary.

"But finally, to accommodate the British, some of the chiefs sent some of their children to school. My grandfather, for instance, sent his oldest son—my father—to school, just to see what it was all about. Francis Deng was sent by his father, another chief. My father wound up graduating from Columbia University. My grandfather's other sons, my uncles, were not sent to school. They led the traditional life, farming, working with the cattle. I wound up in school because my father had gone to school. My uncles' children did not. If your father did not want you to go to school, you did not go."

The first Dinka students were explorers as surely as if they had set off in Spanish galleons toward a strangely curved horizon. They started young, at the missionary schools, learning this English language under the Lutherans or the Catholics or learning Arabic under the Muslims, leaving for Khartoum and the university and leaving Khartoum for the libraries of the Western world. They were explorers and they were exceptions.

The typical Dinka father, uneducated himself, saw no virtue in school. He wanted his sons to lead the Dinka life with Dinka values. Horizons were not interesting. Cows were interesting and village life was interesting and talk, long into the night, everyone telling stories until one by one the audience fell asleep was interesting. A book will not tell you how to elude a lion, how to fashion a spear, how to feed a family. Education was gained by listening to the wisdom of others, by living. God in the sky and all the gods in the ground knew this. The typical Dinka father knew this.

Manute's father was a typical Dinka father.

"Many people were hostile to education," Dr. Francis Deng says. "They were afraid, simply because this was an alien, unknown institution. They were afraid of the effects it might have on their culture, where people did not leave, where they lived the traditional Dinka life."

The father in Dinka society was a beloved autocrat. Mothers did most of the early at-home raising of children, along with all of the cooking, sewing, and cleaning work of the household, yet the father was the person in the family to be given the most respect. He was always to be called "Father," and never to be disobeyed. Mothers were to be called by their names, never "Mother," and could be engaged in daily argument. This did not make them second-class citizens in Dinka thinking, although that was how they would be perceived in the Western world. This was their traditional lot, the boundaries of daily living drawn in lines far more definite than in Western society. Men would not do women's work. Women would not do men's work. Period.

The father was in charge of the cattle, the farm, the outdoors livelihood. He was also the decision maker. With as many as two hundred wives in some bizarre and wealthy circumstances, he might not even know all of his children. He might only remember them when they told him the names of their mothers. This did not interfere with decisions. He was still the person who made the decisions, the man to be obeyed and honored.

Madut Bol, Manute's father, was the son of Bol Chol, the seven-foot-ten chief with the forty wives and more than eighty children. Bol Chol was the head of the Amyol branch of the Tuich branch of the Dinka. Edward Bona describes the position as akin to being the legal head of a tremendous family—say, "all the Murphys in the world"—but more than that. The family had great prestige, great tradition. Maybe all the Kennedys in the world. The chief was the all-powerful ruler. There were no written laws, no governing bodies in Dinka society. He was in charge. He settled all disputes. His decisions were final, immutable. He counseled the sick, officiated at tribal rituals. He was the final legal, political, educational, religious, medical authority. He was everything.

Madut Bol, standing six feet eight, retained some of his father's grand reputation. He was, after all, like a Kennedy, a special person from a special family. He owned a large number of cows, the sign of wealth. He settled local disputes. His home was in Turalie, a far-flung village on the northwestern edge of the Sudd, the world's largest swamp. The village was large, spread out, somewhere between five thousand and ten thousand people in the loosely defined region between two tributaries of the Nile River. The way of life was mostly unchanged from the way of life of years ago, primitive and tied to the forces of nature. No electricity. No cars. No newspapers. Thatched mud huts. When the rainy season flooded the rivers from April to December, and turned the land into muck, the cows were taken to higher ground. The jungle animals of Tarzan movies flourished. The many mosquitoes brought disease and sudden death. This was the basic symbiotic relationship between man and environment.

"I tell people in the United States how we lived and they can't comprehend," Edward Bona says. "They don't believe you can live without the things of society. No electricity? They don't know. This was real. And it was good. It was a life I think any Dinka, no matter how educated he becomes, always wishes he still had in a lot of ways. I know I do."

The second of Madut Bol's seven wives was named Okwok. She twice gave birth to stillborn twins, and there were worries that she might never have children. Madut and Okwok went to a chief, a Master of the Fishing Spear, with their problem. This was a traditional recourse. Dinka belief was that if there was a problem with child-bearing, certain gods in the ground must be unhappy. The Master of the Fishing Spear had to be consulted. He told Madut and Okwok they would, indeed, have a healthy child and that it would be a boy and that they should name him Manute. In the Dinka language, this means "Special Blessing." The boy, as predicted, was born. He was given the name.

His early life followed familiar Dinka patterns. From the age of four, he herded sheep and goats with the other boys of his age.

He learned the oral language, the oral traditions. The goal of the boys his age was the initiation ceremony, the removal of teeth at seven or eight, the markings at eleven or twelve, the age when boys became men and began to herd cattle. There was no mention of school. Madut Bol did not believe in school. The problem was that his son did. Even then.

"I want to go," he told his father.

"No," Madut Bol said. "It is too far. You should be here."

"I will go anyway," Manute said.

"No you won't."

What to do? This seemed to underline the bad influences of civilization. As Manute grew older, closer to the initiation rites, he became rebellious. He did not particularly want the markings and definitely did not want his teeth removed. He did want education. A conflict developed in his mind that has still not been totally resolved, no matter how much he has accomplished. Should he follow his father's wishes? Should he follow his own interests? What? He ran away from home.

"So what is happening is that I run away to a town Abyei," he told Blaine Harden of *The Washington Post* for an article later reprinted in a book entitled *Africa, Dispatches from a Fragile Continent* that chronicled much of his Dinka life. "It was a two-day walk [about thirty-five miles north]. My grandfather got a friend in Abyei, a sell-man [merchant] who let me stay with him. I went there to go to school. I was very young, nine or ten. I stayed there for about a week, but then my father came and took me back. When I was eleven or twelve, I left home again. My father didn't find me this time. I came to a place called Babanusa [about 150 miles north of Turalie, in Arabic-speaking Sudan]. I tried to go to school. I couldn't make it. I didn't speak Arabic good enough."

This time, after a year away, selling peanuts and clothing in Babanusa, he returned to Turalie to submit to the rituals and the life. His mother had died of unknown causes while he was gone, and so now, as her oldest and only son, he was expected to take care of his younger sister, Abouk. He mended relations with his father. He submitted to the knife and the extraction of his teeth, one after another, his head shaved and rubbed with ashes for the ceremony. He was a Dinka man, about fourteen years old, and headed for the cattle camp and the milk-drinking *toc* and the other parts of Dinka life. He was going to be no different from any of his forefathers, tied to his cows and his homeland, ready to marry and marry again (and again) and to begin to accumulate his local wealth. He would learn how to fight at the cattle camp in various warlike sports involving clubs and rocks. He would learn the ways of the cattle and teach them to his many children, prosper and grow old and die. He was another member of the tribe in all ways.

Except he was tall. Very tall.

"I grew up mostly in Khartoum, but often we would travel to the south to see my grandparents in the village," Edward Bona says. "I had met my cousin when he was five or six years old. I suppose he was tall for his age, but that was no surprise. Many of us Dinka are tall, with long legs. I thought nothing of it. Then, one year, my father went south. He was the minister of culture and when he traveled he would stop in the various villages to see his constituency. Campaigning, I guess you would say. He went this time with my uncle. They stopped in Turalie and someone from the press was with them, because my father was a high official. The person from the press took a picture of my father, my uncle, and Manute. It was published in the paper in Khartoum."

The picture showed that Manute had grown to be an enormous young man. The Dinka, yes, were large people. They called themselves *monyjang*, which means men of men. The British called them Ghostly Giants. Manute was more ghostly than the other giants. Or more gigantic than the other ghosts. Or something. Seven feet seven. He dominated the picture, the tallest man imaginable.

"I was playing basketball then for the national team in Khartoum," Edward Bona says. "I remember we had the paper and all of us were just laughing. Looking at this guy. Thinking about what he could do as a basketball player. Someone said, 'Hey, we've got to get this guy up here.'"

A succession of starts and stops now began. The picture was widely circulated. The great lure of height was irresistible, even in Africa. An uncle convinced the police chief in Wau, the biggest city in the south, maybe eighty thousand people, to invite Manute to play for the police team. Manute had never heard of this game, this basketball. This was 1979. To put the date in perspective, this was the year Magic Johnson and Larry Bird were finishing their college careers in the NCAA finals and about to begin their professional careers in the fall. Manute had never heard of basketball.

He walked the sixty-mile distance to the big city in three days, his first trip to Wau. This was not an excessive amount of walking for a Dinka; they walked everywhere, not for fitness but for transportation, routinely walking for three or four hours simply to meet friends, share conversation for an early evening, then turn around and walk three or four hours home. In Wau, Manute listened to the offer, thought it sounded silly and walked home. Three more days. A game with a ball? His father also did not like the idea of playing basketball.

A cousin, a pilot for Sudan Airlines, Joseph Victor Bol Bol, next went to Turalie to explain the possibilities. He talked about America, about money, about fame. For playing basketball. Basketball? The idea still sounded silly, but Manute went back with his cousin to Wau. He played the game for the first time, in bare feet, outdoors. He tried to control the out-of-control bouncing ball. He tried a little shooting. He still wasn't really interested, until a few days later when his cousin encouraged him to try to dunk the ball. Why not? Seven feet seven. He jumped. He knocked out two of his upper teeth on the rim. Another initiation rite.

"That made me mad," he reported. "I said, 'I'm going to learn this thing.' I began practicing hard."

When yet another cousin, Nyoul Makwag Bol, a guard on the national team, came down with an offer to play for the Catholic Club in Khartoum, Manute was ready to go. They took the train with another player from Wau.

"I had gone to Fordham by the time Manute arrived," Edward Bona says. "Which was too bad. It had been a lot of fun at the Catholic Club. You'd play, you'd hang around. All the Dinka were there. It was a nice club. On Thursday nights, they'd show movies. Set up a screen on the outdoor court. Set up the chairs. All the families would come. There was a little snack bar where you could buy something to eat. We'd talk and laugh.

"There were a few of us who had been around, played for the national team, who would have helped. But we all seemed to go somewhere before he got there. It was a time, suddenly you could go farther than you'd ever thought. First, the dream was maybe to go to Egypt, play ball there. Now, suddenly, it was America. Play ball in America. Play in the NBA. That's what guys were thinking."

Away from the cows. Off toward the thing called "What."

Michael Malouk Wiet was one of the players still in Khartoum when his cousin arrived. Michael and Manute had never met, but both knew they were related by the genealogical charts that each Dinka carries in his head. Michael was no different from anyone else: He was astounded by his cousin's size.

"We already had a tall team, but Manute was impossible," he says. "I am six feet eight, no more than sixth or seventh tall man on the team, but I was still the center on the team until Manute came. I remember, he could not dribble a ball when he came. He would just get the rebound and pass. You could go right by him on defense. He didn't know anything. Six months later, he is on the national team and I am not the center."

Michael also grew up in a small town in the south, but with a father who valued education. He learned English and Arabic at an early age and moved along to study at the University of Khartoum. He was already on the alternate Dinka track to the future, the city mouse welcoming the country mouse to the new environment. He and Manute played on the same teams, did most of the same things, except every afternoon Michael went to school and Manute hung around, killing time.

The practices were in the early mornings, then again in the early evenings to escape the heat. Manute and Michael and the other players would play table tennis in their free time, walk around the city, go to movies. Manute would sit in the front row, on the aisle, his legs spread out toward the screen. He liked cowboy movies. He liked action. There were even some films at the Catholic Club of the NBA in action. Manute got his first actual look at where he was trying to go.

"I remember him looking at Kareem Abdul-Jabbar," Michael says. "Manute said, 'I am taller than him. I can be better than him.' That was the way he thought. We all got along fine. Manute had some trouble with the Arabs, making fun of him, but they began to respect him. He had fights with them. A lot of fights. He had one fight with a bus driver. Manute would stand on the steps because he was so tall, and the bus driver wanted him to move. Manute wouldn't move. They had a fight. Manute was a good fighter."

One large memory is a trip to America that was never made. The national team was scheduled to go to Fort Bragg, North Carolina. Michael and Manute were part of the team. A lot of talk, a lot of planning surrounded that trip. How much fun would it be? Michael promised a girlfriend he would bring her back some dresses and shoes from America. He saw himself coming back wearing a large cowboy hat. The coach asked

Michael and Manute to meet him for lunch. At lunch he informed them that they were not on the roster for the trip. The explanations were political, something about having to mix players from the north and the south, about straightening out an overall roster that had eight centers. He said he could take only four centers. The explanations seemed like nonsense.

"I say today that Manute did not go because he'd had a fight with another player," Michael says. "Manute says this isn't so, but it is. Manute had a fight. That is why the coach didn't take him to America. The coach didn't take me because I had skipped a couple of practices. It was awful. My girlfriend started crying because she wasn't going to get these gifts. Manute and I, we didn't want to come out on the street. I told my girlfriend, in the end, 'Hey, this is life.' I still don't think she understood."

Michael also missed Manute's ultimate break to America. By that time, Michael had moved to Egypt to play semi-pro basketball for the Zemalek Club. This was the old-line hope, basketball in Cairo. Manute was moving to another level, traveling with Deng Nihal, another teammate. Michael often thinks that he could have been a third in the group, off on that adventure, then tells himself he is satisfied with what has happened in his own life. He is close to his country and family. He has a wife and will have more. He is close to America. He works in part of America every day, this giant American building with its armed guards and their nervousness in the midst of the smells and sounds and the enormous numbers of people of the Middle East. He is even close to Manute, who comes back every summer. What could be better? Only one thing.

"Someday," Michael Malouk says, "we will even be able to go home. Someday."

An embassy official stops him in the hall. They talk for a bit about dealings in the office and then the embassy official mentions that the United Nations is planning to resume flights of food and medical supplies back to the refugees in the camps in the south of Sudan. This is significant because the flights had stopped after a Red Cross plane was shot down in the area a month earlier. Both sides in the war claimed the other side was responsible. Who knows?

"Just tell your people," the embassy official says, "this is friendly. Don't shoot this one down."

The giant learned to do tricks with the round ball. He found that he was so tall he could do tricks that no one else could do. His friends were amazed. They told him that he would become famous because of his tricks.

The giant was not sure.

Could this be?

Tony Amin is looking for the tall kid. The new kid. His name is Dud. No one seems to know his second name. Just Dud. Not Dud Tongal. A new kid. He is supposed to be as tall as Manute. No, maybe not as tall, but close. Within a few centimeters. The kid showed up in Khartoum from the south, a Dinka, same as Manute. Plays at the Catholic Club, same as Manute. Tony Amin thinks the kid might be better than Manute at this stage—a little heavier, a little more coordination. Where is this kid? No one seems to know.

"Go find Dud," he says in Arabic to the various Dinka men he meets at the military basketball court behind the train station. "Tell him I want to see him."

It is early evening in Khartoum. A basketball tournament is taking place, high school teams on the black-and-white tiled court that looks so wrong to a Western eye. Who builds a court with the same tiles you would use to cover, say, a public space outside city hall? The backboards are wooden, from another era. The ball that is being used is one of those inexpensive Mikasa balls, rubber, a ball that threatens to bounce off the hard tile and out of any dribbler's fingers at any moment. One team is from Khartoum. The other team is visiting from Port Sudan. Tony Amin seems to know everyone.

"I would like to get this kid, Dud, to America," he says. "There is nothing more he can learn here. He cannot get better here. He should go to America. I just don't know how that can happen. How do you do it? It is like a miracle to get to America. I wrote a letter to your senator, Bill Bradley, six months ago, about Dud. I once read Bill Bradley's book *A Sense of Where You Are*. Maybe he can help. Six months. I have not heard from him."

Amin is forty-five years old, heavy, with a large mustache. He was born in Khartoum, has lived his entire life here, but his family came from Greece. He is single, a basketball bachelor, one of those characters who keep the game moving at the bottom level everywhere it is played. He coaches, he referees, he putters and schemes inside the local basketball society. Look in the back of his jeep on a given day and you can find balls, nets, uniforms, and a couple of point guards who need a ride to the game. He thrives on the local jealousies and confrontations. His day job as an accountant at the Nile Paint Company is work. Basketball is life. He could be living in a small town in Indiana, dreaming forever of sending a kid to Bob Knight at State U. Instead, he lives here, in the capital of this country in the midst of civil war, a Coptic Christian in a Muslim land, coaching mostly Dinkas, kids from the wrong side of the war, refugees from the south where the fighting and famine are everywhere. He dreams of sending a kid to America. Another kid.

"This kid does things Manute couldn't do," Amin says. "He shoots much better than Manute. Then again, Manute . . . ah, Manute."

The game on the court has ended. Amin talks with the referees, his friends. The kids from Port Sudan move to the stands as another game begins, two local teams. Not one of the kids from Port Sudan has actual sneakers. The kids wear instead some kind of low black casual canvas shoe that might have been made thirty years ago for retirees in their golden Florida years. Sneakers are a big problem in Sudan. No one wears the modern, advertised, jump-out-of-the-playground shoes. Not available. A lot of things are not available here. The numbers on the Port Sudan kids' green shirts have been drawn neatly with a felt-tipped pen. High school uniforms. The kids talk in the quiet, muted way of losers. The language is Arabic.

"It is sad, what they say," Amin says.

What is that?

"They lost the game, 31–0," Amin says. "They didn't score a point. They are talking about how different it is when they come here to play where there are nets on the rims and nice balls and referees. That is sad, 31–0. No points at all. They have come a long way from Port Sudan."

The telephone system in Khartoum is terrible. There is no telephone book, no way to look up a number or an address. Amin says there was a telephone book a while ago, but he cannot remember when. It does not seem to matter much because there are few phones and there seem to be no addresses. Directions are given by noting a landmark and counting off streets or houses. Communication is mostly through acquaintances. Looking for someone? Go to a certain place he might be. If he is not there, ask the people who are there if they have seen him. The Muslim term for every occurrence in life is *in shala*, God's will. Maybe someone will take you to him, maybe not. *In shala.*

"Come on," Amin says. "We will go to the Catholic Club in my jeep. We will look for Dud. I will show you where Manute lived."

This is Friday, the Muslim Sabbath, so there is not much traffic on the main streets of the city. On a normal day, especially in the early morning and the late afternoon, the streets are filled with an exotic parade of people and vehicles and animals. Women, as required by Muslim law, wear the head covering, but in this country the fabrics are colorful prints, matching the women's ankle-length dresses. Arab men wear white, topped with exaggerated foot-high turbans. Historic speculation is that the turbans are so tall because the men are much shorter than the Dinka. The Arabs say this is not so. The Dinka men and the Nuer and the members of the other Nilotic tribes wear virtually anything, the long robes of the Middle East or outdated Western clothes. Buses are crowded to double, triple their capacities. Flat-bed trucks are filled in the back with women, children, men. People as cargo, maybe one hundred people, maybe two hundred on the back of a truck. Burros walk next to buses. Burros, goats, dogs. Small, frail children, obviously unwashed for the longest time, approach strangers for pound notes. Everything is played against a sandy brown background. Sand on the streets. Sand on the sides of the buildings. Sand in the air, dust storms coming straight from the desert. Black skin is put against a brown environment. Many of the faces have the tribal scars; different scars for different branches of different tribes. Men and women have the scars. On the older, lighter-skinned faces the scars on the cheeks sometimes look like tracks of tears, as if the person has been crying.

"Manute had trouble with the people when he first came here," Amin says as he drives over the now-quiet streets. "People would run after him, yell things, make fun of his size. He used to walk with a big, carved stick. If people said too much, he would swing the stick at them. He would hit a lot, too. The people would not calculate right. The long arms, the length of the stick—they would think they were free, but they were still within his reach."

The presence of the military is felt everywhere. Trucks filled with soldiers pass. Soldiers stand guard at the front doors of hotels, checking the packages and handbags of everyone who enters. The soldiers are dressed in light green, the police in a darker shade. Each of them seems to carry an automatic weapon. The war so far has been confined to the south, the conflict now reduced to the Dinka guerrillas against the Muslim government and its allied tribes, but Dinka leader John Garang has promised that Khartoum will be involved sometime in the future. There is an 11:00 P.M. curfew for everyone and various restrictions have been put into effect. Photographs are forbidden without obtaining a permit from the police station. Even with the permit, a visitor cannot photograph government buildings, roads, bridges, strategic locations of any sort, scenes of poverty, and so on. A person, basically, cannot take a picture of anything. The few phones are supposedly tapped for overseas calls. The hotel staff and the cabdrivers are supposedly informers for the police. Paranoia is not an unknown feeling where there are perpetual stories of imprisonment and torture and execution.

"This is the train station," Amin says. "This is where the train would go to Wau, to the south, where Manute lived. There are no trains now. The war. Only military trains."

The Dinka refugees from the south are on the low end of the social ladder. Historically, this has been a poor country—run by the Turks and the Egyptians and the English and other forces during colonial times, known in Arabic as *Bilad-as-Sudan*, Land of the Blacks—and it is even poorer now. There is little industry, few signs of any of the familiar logos of the free world. No McDonald's. No General Motors. No famous banks. The country has a total external debt of $14 billion, nearly twice the gross domestic product, and owes the International Monetary Fund $1 billion, the organization's largest outstanding debt. The Muslim military government was on the side of Iraq during the Gulf War and that seemed to clinch the West's lack of interest. Who should care about Sudan? There are reports that Khartoum has become one of the prime bases for international terrorists, a perfect place to hide. Who cares? An always-forgotten land has become even more forgotten.

The Dinka, easily recognizable, are the blackest people in the city, probably the blackest people in the world. There is little work for the Dinka, little housing. Many of them are urban nomads, sleeping where they can, often under the stars. How do they eat? How do they live? Three young guys hanging around the airport, doing nothing for another day, had answered the question earlier. "As they say around here," one of the Dinka said with a little smile, "*in shala.*" At least they are better off than the refugees at the camps on the other side of the river. The camps are overcrowded, with more refugees arriving daily, escaping from the troubles of the south. There are rumors that the government is simply going to close the camps, to send the refugees back to the places they have left.

A story is told about the last time Manute visited, after he had made the money and become famous. He stayed in a penthouse at one of the best hotels in the city, one logo that is here on the banks of the Nile. The Dinka heard he was in the city, this most famous Dinka of all by now, and people went to see him. Friends. Relations. Supplicants. A line of Dinka formed outside his door as if he were a chief, a potentate, a godfather who might dispense favors. Hotel management became nervous. Too many blacks— very black—faces were going through the lobby. Shade somehow was as important here in the Land of the Blacks as it would be in South Africa. Lighter black was the norm; the Muslim blacks do not even call themselves black; they use the terms *red* and *blue* and *green*. Very black was embarrassing. Hotel management asked Manute to leave. That was the story.

"I have worked with the Dinka for a long time," Amin says, pulling the jeep to the front of the Catholic Club. "This is where they come to play basketball and to hang around when they come to this city. This is their social base. I have found them to be very intelligent people. I think anyone will tell you that about the Dinka, that they are very intelligent people. But they are having a tough time now. Life is hard for them."

The club is the first building a visitor will see when he exits from the old airport parking lot. The name is written across the doorway in green letters. Catholic Club. Welcome to Sudan. A Catholic club in a Muslim country.

The war has been percolating since 1983, becoming worse and worse in each succeeding year. It is called the Second Civil War. The First Civil War began in 1955, with the arrival of independence from the British, and continued until 1972. The issues mainly have remained the same, the Muslim government of the north trying to impose its law on the Nilotic tribes of the south. There have been no real battle lines, the Khartoum government controlling the major cities of the south—Wau and Juba—and the tribal guerrillas mostly controlling the countryside. Violence seems almost random, without strategy, massacres of entire villages by either side, no advantage gained in either direction.

A report on CNN only two nights earlier in Cairo—the night Michael Malouk was describing basketball at the Catholic Club—said that a massacre had been discovered in the southern town of Bor, perhaps seven thousand people killed, most of them Dinka. The placement of the report in the international broadcast somehow said as much about the situation as the report itself: The lead story concerned a helicopter crash in Europe, five dead. The second story detailed fighting in Tblisi, Georgia. The third story showed U.S. President George Bush becoming sick to his stomach at a state dinner in Japan.

"Coming up next," the anchorman said, "tribal violence leaves thousands dead in southern Sudan."

There was a pause for a commercial citing the benefits of a Mitsubishi truck. The anchorman returned, gave a warning about the "graphic" pictures that would be shown, then launched into the story. The fourth story of the news. Seven thousand dead. The incident had happened as long as a month ago. Seven thousand dead. The announcer said many women and children had been kidnapped and that this was the largest tribal massacre ever. Fourth story on the news, following a case of indigestion for the president of the United States and a commercial. Third World problems. Low-rent news. Violence in a vacuum.

Even the people in Khartoum did not know this had happened and did not seem shocked that it had. Or maybe they did not believe it. The few televisions in Khartoum show a never-ending discussion of the precepts of Islam. No CNN.

"You do not know about this?" a visitor would ask.

"No," was the constant reply.

"You have heard nothing?"

"No."

A representative of Amnesty International in Washington, D.C., had said that all of the civil wars in Africa, except the troubles in South Africa, were happening in this kind of vacuum. Who knew? Who cared? The relaxation of the cold war had brought a new level of unconcern about the region. The United States and the Soviet Union no longer were running around the continent, propping up various regimes in the battle for allies against either communism or capitalism. That big battle seemed done, everyone returning home—but leaving the toys of war behind. The toys were being used now with a vengeance and nobody seemed to notice.

There was a civil war in Somalia, another in Chad. Refugees from the Sudan were going into Ethiopia, but then refugees from Ethiopia had fled not long ago into the Sudan. A look at the map of Sudan and its neighbors was a look at turmoil. Zaire to the south. Uganda. The precolonial divisions in language or culture or religion or whatever were now hardened into conflict, everyone free to address these long-forgotten issues.

The disputes in the Sudan were influenced by all of these

factors. The country is large, one-third the size of the United States, the largest country on the continent. There is little doubt, logically, that the country should be divided in half, but logic has never been a large geopolitical consideration anywhere. The north is mostly desert, mostly Arab, almost an extension of the Middle East. The south is mostly swamp, mostly Nilotic tribes, an extension of the black heart of Africa. The Arabs see the tribes of the south as intellectual inferiors, religious heathens. The tribes see the Arabs as invaders.

The eleven-year peace between 1972 and 1983—luckily timed to allow the children of Manute's Dinka generation to grow up without becoming statistics in the conflict—was an uneasy alliance between the two sides. When the Muslim government of Jaafer al Nimeiri decided in 1983 to make Islam the official religion and imposed the strict Islamic law known as *sharia* through the region, the peace fell apart. The Sudan People's Liberation Movement was formed under Garang and the war began again, becoming uglier and uglier.

Amnesty International, though it does not rank countries in numbers of violations, cites the Sudan as one of the world's largest trouble spots. The group's pamphlet of August 1990, entitled "Sudan, A Permanent Human Rights Crisis," talks about secret detention centers in Khartoum called "ghost houses," and about public floggings and amputations and crucifixions. The pamphlet cites atrocities on both sides of the conflict.

"On one side you have Muslim fundamentalism," one Khartoum intellectual says. "This is a jihad, a holy war. If a soldier dies, he dies with great honor and goes straight to his heaven. On the other side, you have people defending their land, where they have always lived, defending their way of life. How does a war like this ever end? How do two sides get together? Both are so committed to what they are doing."

The economy, already destroyed, sinks even deeper. The best-educated citizens become either political leaders or expatriates, bringing their learning to markets that have less need. A backward country slips farther backward. "The Sudan is a useless possession, ever was so, and ever will be so. . . . " Britain's General Gordon wrote before his 1885 demise. "No one who has ever lived in the Sudan can escape the reflection, 'What a useless possession is this land.' Few men can stand its fearful monotony and deadly climate." The people who live here do not agree. The fighting continues.

"It is all just terrible in the south," a Dinka cabdriver, who does not want his name used, says in the quiet of a January night. "You cannot describe how terrible it is."

He explains the life he once lived in the south. His father had five wives. Both his father and mother had the tribal scars. His father had two stripes on the sides of his head. His mother had stripes down her cheeks. His mother was from a tribe in the west of Sudan, his father from the center of the country.

"Each tribe wanted its own world, wanted to know its own people," the driver says. "This is the way to do it. Some of the tribes from the west had a large V on their cheeks. It was something that everybody did at one time.

"I lived in a village, like Manute, in a house made of sticks, the grass growing over the roof. The rain would come and roll right off. We had a gas light, that's all. The animals were everywhere. We would see the lions in the jungle, the elephants, everything. The snakes. Too many snakes. We would drink the milk. The milk dare? How much milk you could drink? The *toc*? We would do that. We would drink milk and eat grain and fish. In the winter, when the cows would go in the jungle, that was when we would eat fish. You would just go to the river. No problem. There were a lot of fish."

The driver said the timelessness of the life was perfect, but this was the life that disappeared when the war started. Where is it now? Gone. The driver talks in a subdued voice. He came to Khartoum as a refugee.

"Now, the animals are dead in the south. The little children, too. It is terrible," he says. "My parents have moved to a town

near the border in Ethiopia. I hope that they are all right. I don't
know. There is no way to be in contact."

The driver's ambition has become a variant of Manute's: to
move, to go to the West, to go to America. His chances of getting
there are much slimmer because he is about five feet ten inches
tall. No one is coming along to help. He does not know how to
play basketball. He says he has applied for a visa at the American
embassy but knows that is hopeless. No one is getting American
visas. His idea is to move somewhere else, an intermediate country, somewhere he can work and put together some money and
find a more favorable situation for getting a visa.

"I have tried this once already," he says. "I moved to another
country. Unfortunately, the country was Kuwait. I was there two
years. I had a job, I had saved a lot of money. Then the invasion
came. What could I do? My money was in the bank. The Iraqis
took everything. All I could do was escape with my life. I mostly
walked across all of Iraq to Jordan, then came back here. Here I
am, saving money again to move somewhere else. I will do it."
In shala.

"Have you seen Dud?" Amin asks a Dinka named Peter in
English.

"Dud was here last night, darling," Peter says, a familiar form
from some other language somehow brought into his knowledge
of this one. "He has not been around tonight."

"Can someone go look for him?"

"I will send someone, darling."

The building in the front of the club grounds contains a recreation room with a Ping-Pong table and a pool table. It resem-
bles the recreation room at an American YMCA. A bulletin
board at the entrance has a four-color basketball picture, ripped
from some magazine. Oddly enough, it is a picture of Charles
Barkley, with guard Rickey Green in the background. The Six-

ers. Manute's team. There is no picture of Manute. There are two basketball courts behind the building, an old court and a newer one. The older one has a floor of cracked cement. The newer one has the strange tiles. Some kids are playing a three-on-three game on the newer court. The baskets have been ripped off the backboards on the older court. This is the court where Manute played. Games have not been played on this court for a while.

"See that bench?" Amin says. "That is where I made Manute sit. He came here and he wanted to play right away. I told him to sit. He sat and he sat for two months during the games. I would not let him play. I thought he was lazy. I wanted him to want to play. I was waiting for him to say something. Finally, he came to me and asked why he wasn't playing. He said he wanted to play. That was all I had to hear. He played the next game and he never stopped. I could not take him out."

Amin heard about Manute from Nyoul Makwag Bol, one of the cousins who had encouraged Manute to play basketball in the first place. Amin was intrigued. The dream, of course. He had his own team in the local semi-professional league. The players did not receive much—£S2 per month—but the competition was as good as could be found in all of the Sudan. Nyoul Makwag Bol said Manute should come and live in Khartoum and develop and play for Amin and, later perhaps, the national team. Manute could be that good. Amin was intrigued.

He purchased two tickets on the train to Wau so Nyoul Makwag Bol and a teammate could find Manute and bring him back. A third ticket was sent along for Manute. The three tickets cost £S28 total, the equivalent then of six American dollars. Amin paid from club funds.

"They came back at night and we made a bed on the floor of this storage shed in the back of the club for Manute," Amin says. "He was tired and went right to sleep. There was a guard who checked the grounds every night. He checked the shed and saw Manute on the floor. The Sudanese like to sleep totally covered, head and everything. The guard came running to my house and said there was a dead body on the floor of the shed, that I had to come. I told him there was nothing wrong, but I went anyway. We looked in the shed. We made some noise. Manute woke up. He stood up, with all the bedclothes around him. The guard had not realized how big Manute was. He saw this giant man rise off the ground and thought he had seen a spirit. He screamed and ran from the shed. Manute did not know what was going on."

Manute was raw, but Amin realized as a coach he had something no one else in Khartoum had, a basketball player of a size that could not be imagined. He offered Manute a contract of £S15 per month, far above the £S2 offered to the other players, and told Manute to keep the figure secret. Included was lodging in the shed and free meals every day in a restaurant downtown. The deal with the restaurant was that patrons could watch him eat as a word-of-mouth advertised attraction—not as a basketball player, but as an extremely tall person. An oddity. The shed for living was basic, a place where lawn mowers and equipment were stored. The national tennis center, with genuine grass courts, was next door. Manute would sleep with the equipment and be awakened by the plop, plop of tennis balls being hit outside the walls.

"You can see the shed, not much different from the way it was then," Amin says, opening the door. "He did not have much. When he came here all he had was the one *jalabiah* [dressing gown] and a small handbag containing two underwear only. The sandals on his feet."

Amin opens the door to the shed. Little light penetrates. Graffiti is on the walls, the names "Michael Jackson" and "Boul" written in black paint. No one lives here now, possibly no one since Manute did. Some broken-down lawn equipment sits on the floor. Amin says he built a special bed for Manute and this was home. It looks now as if it is used by young boys as a secret club or meeting place, nothing more. Amin says Manute moved, after a while, into an apartment on the other side of the club. A man is barbecuing a piece of lamb on an old grill on the apartment's wooden steps. His daughter watches.

"Manute was bothered about his height when he was here," Amin says. "All of the people making fun of him. He was always fighting. He would throw rocks at people. They would throw rocks at him. I told him he should not be bothered. I said, 'You did not create yourself. You were created by God. You should laugh at everyone else because they are so short. That is what you should do.' "

Amin found special pants for his new player, plus sneakers. The sneakers were too small, but sneakers were always a problem. Manute's feet today are curled and painful-looking because of his history of too-small sneakers. There was not one pair of size 15½ sneakers in all of Sudan. He sometimes played in his bare feet.

On the court, Amin says Manute had to start from the virtual beginning. He did not jump at all. He was not aggressive. Amin talked to him about two things. The first was blocking shots. This was going to be Manute's strength. He should block any shot possible and if he missed the ball, he should not miss the man; let the referees decide what's legal and what isn't. The second thing was that Manute should watch from the sidelines and see how the ball was distributed from the top of the key. See? When he played, he should go inside and make himself available for the ball. See? He should stuff the ball into the basket when he got it. Maybe even jump. He did not have to dribble, do a lot of parts of the game. Block shots. Stuff the ball. Rebound. That would be fine.

"And then we played," Amin says. "He paid attention. He got better and better. Who could stop him? We were dropping special balls for him, just throwing to him. He was too big. We beat everyone. I always wanted a low-scoring game, but we got too many baskets. We could not stop. We beat one team and their coach said, 'Manute, he is a million and we are nothing.' "

The Catholic Club became the power of the Khartoum league. Manute eventually also joined the Sudanese national team. To do this, he had to join the army, where he was listed as a paratrooper, of all things. He never had to jump out of a plane, just jump for the rebounds. The national team took him outside the country for the first time, traveling to games in Saudi Arabia, Egypt, Algeria, and Italy. By now, Manute had heard about the NBA and had even seen films of NBA games. Julius Erving, "Doctor J," was his favorite, playing with the Sixers. Going to America was a definite ambition.

The national team, as Michael Malouk said, suddenly scheduled a game in Fort Bragg, North Carolina. Going to America? The coach—as Michael Malouk also said—announced that Manute would not be on this traveling team.

"The coach . . . I still do not believe it," Tony Amin says. "I ask him, 'Why aren't you taking Manute?' The coach says Manute is not good enough. He does not hold onto the ball. I tell him, 'If you are any kind of a coach, you should know better.' I still talk to him about this. I say, 'What do you think now, you are here and Manute is in the States?' "

Manute believed—still believes—that the reason he was not on the trip was that the coach was afraid he would leave the team once he got to the States. He says the coach knew that some college scout would see him and Manute would have been gone. Which was the truth. He would have been gone.

As it was, he left the team and returned to the south. He didn't know what to do. Should he make his father happy and live his father's life? Was he doomed in this idea of going to America? While he was considering his options, thinking he probably was going to return to Khartoum and basketball and prove the coach wrong, someone heard on a radio somewhere that an American coach had arrived to coach the national team in the summer. This clinched Manute's decision. He started walking toward Wau again and the train station.

* * *

The dream that he could go to America, to play in the NBA, was, of course, totally unrealistic. Especially for Manute. No education. No basketball background. America?

Eleven years have passed since Manute started walking back from Wau, and the dream is still on the far edge of reality. An African-qualifying tournament is being held in Cairo for the 1992 Olympics at the same time Amin tells his story. The best players, the eleven best national teams in the entire continent, have gathered at the 25,000-seat Cairo Sports Complex in Nasr City. America? There will be a tough time finding a team suitable to send to Barcelona.

"There is just so much to overcome in African basketball," a twenty-four-year-old American named Craig Madzinski says, watching Mali and the Central African Republic roll through a turnover-filled forty minutes. "The possibilities for basketball are unbelievable, but no one in America can understand the problems. It is all so different."

The games are ragged affairs. The Arabic teams from the north of Africa—Egypt, Morocco, Algeria, and Tunisia—play a patterned, European style of basketball, relying on plays and 3-point shooting. The black teams from the south—Senegal, Nigeria, Mali, Angola, Ivory Coast, the Central African Republic, and Cameroon—play a free-form, inner-city U.S. game. There are a number of tall players, players who have played at American colleges or professionally in Europe, so the action around the basket is very good. Dunks and blocked shots are common. The difference is in the ballhandling. The dribbling and the ballhandling sometimes are below American high school standards. The ball flies everywhere, each trip up the court an adventure. The fundamentals of the game have not been put together with the obvious bodies for the game.

Madzinski is the coach for a year of the national team of Burundi, a small central African country the size of the state of Maryland. He is scouting the tournament, thinking about possible future games. His own team is still evolving. He says the evolution is slow. This is Africa. If there is no money for food and shelter and roads, how can there be money for sports? There are no facilities in Burundi. There are few pairs of good sneakers. There are no regulation balls. There is no basketball tradition.

"Talent?" he says. "I have seen women in Burundi who are six feet ten. You have these kids . . . you throw the ball out there and it's like throwing a ball in with a bunch of greyhounds. These kids run all day. I have kids who jog four and five miles to come to practice, then jog the same distance back. We don't even have to have warm-up drills. We just get going. These kids jump over the rim without a thought. They're in amazing condition. I have two kids, no sneakers, who can do amazing things. Physically, these kids are as good as any players you would find on any playground in America. They also have no idea of what to do. There isn't one indoor gym in the entire country. The outdoor court we use isn't even regulation. There are no high school teams, no youth programs, no coaches. I am basketball in Burundi. The languages in the country are Kirundi, French, and Swahili, but I say English is the language of basketball. That's all I speak."

He has taken his team on one eleven-game tour of the United States, playing against American small colleges. He talks about the wonders of the experience. Most of his players had never been on an airplane, never had been out of their country. They flew from Bujumbura, Burundi, to Addis Ababa, Ethiopia, to Cairo to Frankfurt, Germany, to Washington, D.C. They practiced at George Washington University. The kids thought they were visiting a palace. A hardwood floor for a basketball court? Leather balls? Glass backboards? They could not believe where they were. This was basketball? These were kids from a place where a small snake can bite your foot and you absolutely know you will be dead in eighteen days because there is no known antidote. Snakes could be understood. Civil war could be understood. Glass backboards?

"We lost all eleven games, of course, but it was a terrific experience," Madzinski says. "We fly all the way back and as I am getting my luggage at the airport, an embassy official meets me and asks if I have heard about the coup attempt. What coup attempt? I go straight home and can't leave for twelve days. There was a curfew at dusk. I could hear gunfire all the time. I would sit on the porch at night and watch firefights. We did all this work in the United States and I haven't seen all of the kids together since we said good-bye at the airport. That's just how it is."

More than one coach at the tournament mentions the "high cost" of basketball. High cost? In America, it is known as a low-budget sport, the best players traditionally coming from the ghettos and rural, farm-boy poverty. In Africa, the game seems almost to be a luxury. Alphonse Bile, the coach of the Ivory Coast, talks about "all the equipment you need for basketball. The rings, the shoes, everything. That is why soccer is such a popular sport in the Third World. I can pick a melon out of a tree, take it to a field and we can have a game of soccer." The Angolan coach, Victorino Silva e Cunha, talks about the lack of good coaches, about present coaches "who are mystics, who believe in Fate, who simply tell their team to go on the floor and God will provide. What chance does mysticism have against a pressure defense?" The Nigerian coach, Toin Sonoiki, talks about the considerations that have to be given to tribes when national teams are built, each tribe in a country represented on the team. A Senegalese player, Guy Gomis, talks about the problem of language: sixty-five different dialects are spoken in his country. Silva e Cunha talks about problems in travel, each game so expensive in his country because it involves an airplane flight since there is no longer any system of roads after twenty years of fighting. Floods are mentioned. Pestilence. Famines. Who can play basketball in the midst of pestilence, of epidemics?

"I don't think they can ever catch up to the United States over here," Jim Calvin, another American coach, says. "It's a shame. You see some of these kids, they're like stallions, running wild. But they're too old by the time you see them. The kids in the

United States are playing basketball when they're eight years old. Here? The kids don't start until they're fourteen and fifteen or even older. And they have no coaches. And they have no tradition."

Calvin, who once coached high school basketball in Indiana and was an assistant at the University of Arkansas at Little Rock, is a club coach in Bahrain in the Persian Gulf. He received a whiff of notoriety in 1990 when he was the coach of the Kuwait national team and Iraq invaded the country. His team's captain was executed, his players were put in jail, and he and his wife and their two dogs escaped in a pell-mell drive to Saudi Arabia. He wound up doing all the talk shows in the United States during the Gulf War, telling his tale. He coached the Rapid City Thrillers in the Continental Basketball Association for the next season, but now is back in the Third World. The different world.

"I read an article in the English-language paper from Saudi Arabia a few weeks ago that tells you how far away you are when you're in the Third World," he says. "It was an interview with the public executioner in Riyadh. They still have the public executions, you know, every Friday. They behead people. They also chop off hands for stealing, stuff like that. This was one of those job-description interviews, nothing supposed to be exciting. The interviewer asks the executioner if he has learned anything on the job. The executioner says indeed he has. He says he has learned that he always has to put the hood over his client's head. He learned this, he says, on the first day of the job. He had two men to execute and he brought them to the stage. Neither wore the hood. They both get down in position for the execution and the executioner chops the first guy's head off. The head, it seems, rolls right under the eyes of the second guy. The second guy sees the head and immediately has a heart attack and dies. The executioner finds that he does not get paid for the second guy, since the second guy was dead already without being executed. Always use the hood. That was the lesson."

Madzinski talks again about basketball talent. He says probably the only way for a Third World kid to succeed in American basketball is to either live in a big African city and move to America for college or, better yet, to move to America as a young boy. He says that is what happened to a six-foot-eight kid from Burundi named Ernest Nzigamasabo. The kid's mother worked at the American embassy and the ambassador at the time was a basketball fan. He arranged for the kid to attend high school in the United States. Nzigamasabo became one of the top 150 prospects in the country and now attends the University of Minnesota on a basketball scholarship.

"That's what you have to do," Madzinski, who was once an assistant at Chicago-Loyola, says. "You look at the players who have made it to the NBA. Hakeem Olajuwon made it moving from Nigeria to Houston. Dikembe Mutombo was from Kinshasa, the biggest city in Zaire. He went to Georgetown for four years before he went to the Denver Nuggets in the pros. You have to get these guys very early to America or they have to come from a big African city. That is the only way."

It is mentioned that there is one other player in the NBA from Africa. Not from a big city. Not from a big city at all.

"Manute," Madzinski says. "Manute is different from everybody. I can't imagine how, coming from where he came from, Manute made it at all. He is from so far away. I can't imagine. And I live in Burundi."

"I forget exactly how he left for America," Tony Amin says. "I know that an American businessman, Elias Stratias, was involved. He had a cousin who works with me at Nile Paint. Stratias came here sometimes on business. He's dead now, I believe, in that crash of Pan Am 103 in Lockerbie, Scotland. I just remember the night Manute left. He had switched to another team in our league. Not the Catholic Club. Deng Nihal, who was going with him to America, was on my team. Nobody knew they were going, except the other coach and me. It was all a big secret. If anyone knew they were going to America to stay, they probably wouldn't have been allowed out of the country.

"Our two teams were playing each other the night the plane left. Everybody was asking where Manute and Deng were. We said they were both sick. They went through the airport and simply told the officials they were going for medical treatment. And they were gone.

"Manute, I remember, was nervous about going. He said to me, 'I have too many cows in the south, maybe I should not leave.' I said, 'You are going to America. Some day you will be so rich you can get the whole cows of the south if you want.' "

The eleven o'clock curfew is approaching. Amin has spent the night looking for the big kid, Dud, but without luck. A last chance was the Dinka souk, the business area, where an outdoor barbecue on top of a garbage can was the only business still open. None of the dark faces in the dark had seen Dud. There is no chance now. The curfew. Amin has not seen an American basketball visitor for a long while and the visitor is leaving. Amin will have to figure out something. He would like Dud to have the chance Manute had.

"He needs coaching," Amin says. "He can learn nothing here. He needs coaching from someone else."

Amin says he thinks he himself may be leaving soon. He is not sure. He has a sister who has emigrated to England and her husband is now preparing to follow, finishing up details in Khartoum. Should Amin do the same? The war is a drain. What is his life here? He has the basketball, but what else? Even the basketball has become more quiet. He does not coach at the Catholic Club, having switched to another club. He did not even have a team in the league this year. What should he do? Talking about

Manute's success has somehow made him sad. He feels far away from everything that is happening.

"At the Catholic Club, you said that the picture on the wall was from the Philadelphia team, the team Manute plays for," Amin says. "I did not even know that he was there. How can that be? I thought he was still with the Washington Bullets."

The American gives Amin a book, as a gift. The book contains a picture of Manute. He is posed with the author of the book at center court of an NBA arena. Manute is wearing a business suit, an arm around the shorter writer. Amin is overwhelmed.

"Look at him," he says. "Wearing that suit. To think what he was wearing when he showed up here . . . "

Amin's voice cracks. He does not finish the sentence.

*One day, a man from the Great Outside appeared.
The man was amazed at the size of the giant, as
everyone was. He also was amazed at the giant's
tricks with the round ball. The man from the Great
Outside said he could make the giant rich and famous. He would get him a ticket. He would bring
him to the Great Outside.*

Somehow.

FEELEY

His business now is ladies' handbags. Don Feeley is not exactly sure how this happened—how he went from basketball to golf to handbags—but it did. Handbags. His second wife was in the business when they were married two years ago and since he had nothing else really happening for him, he is in the business, too. He works from his home in Glastonbury, Connecticut. Handbags. Discount handbags.

"My wife worked a deal yesterday for a thousand dozen handbags," he says. "Isn't that crazy? A thousand dozen. I never knew numbers like that existed. This guy, this distributor, was telling me he made fifty cents on each handbag. A thousand dozen? How much money is that? The money . . . I never thought about the money . . . all I was thinking about was winning games. Isn't that crazy? I never knew this stuff existed. I was worrying about winning some more basketball games."

He is a basketball coach without a team to coach. Handbags? He followed the wrong arrows on the organizational chart and somehow landed here. There was a time when he was wearing his newly cleaned dress suit and trying to decide which of the half-dozen pairs of shoes in the trunk of his car might best impress some search committee for Holy Cross or LaSalle or some reasonably big-time operation. He had a tight little résumé that went from a twenty-game, win-streak season at Andrew Ward High School to thirteen years of Division II success at Sacred Heart University in Bridgeport to two years as an assistant at Yale. Yale! Ivy League! The Division I job he finally landed was at Fairleigh Dickinson College in Rutherford, New Jersey. Three years. What happened at Fairleigh Dickinson? He is fifty-three years old now. He has not coached a college team in seven years. There is gray in his hair and a tired look to his face.

"Philosophical differences with the administration," he says. "That was the problem at Fairleigh Dickinson. I wanted to win. I wanted to go big time. The Meadowlands was right there, waiting down the road. It could have happened. I had North Carolina State, DePaul, Rutgers, Maryland . . . I had all those teams on the schedule and we still finished 17–12. All those losses on the road. Who would play at Fairleigh Dickinson? All the tough games had to be on the road. We still did all right. There just wasn't any support. The president didn't like me . . . the athletic director was a track guy . . . the academic adviser, here was a guy who wasn't there to advise anyone, just to say 'you're ineligible' whenever a kid got in trouble.

"Basketball just didn't seem to count. There was a world champion high jumper, the little guy, Franklin Jacobs. He'd been at the school for five years. He had about twelve credits. Nobody said a thing. It was all so stupid. The AD wouldn't even know the names of the teams we were playing."

What happened? Fairleigh Dickinson was a mistake. There were other ones. A door should have opened somewhere. A proper step should have been made, a different step. What was it? Maybe with Manute. Maybe. That is a thought. Something different could have been done, should have been done. What was it? Manute should have been an answer.

"One of the guys around our program at Fairleigh Dickinson, a trustee, Elias Stratias, had a brother in the Sudan," Feeley says. "Stratias was one of those international businessmen. He eventually died, I believe, in Pan Am Flight 103 over Lockerbie, Scotland. He set it up for me to go over for a month for the State Department to coach the Sudanese national team. It was June, I had nothing going on. I figured I'd do it. He said there might be some players over there for me. I figured I'd take a look."

Feeley had never traveled outside the country. He now went as far outside as he could go. He traveled in 747 luxury, enjoying the meals and the stops in Europe and Egypt. He was not prepared for what awaited. The heat was overpowering. The wind was blowing. The streets were dirt. Paper and refuse and sand flew through the air. He felt as though he had landed in Dodge City in another time. A pair of new sneakers his wife, his first wife, had packed were gone before he left the tiny airport. Mysteriously disappeared during the customs procedure. An army captain met him and drove him to the Excelsior Hotel. The time was two o'clock in the morning.

"I get to the hotel and of course there is no air-conditioning," he says. "I go to my room and can't find the lights. I do see a fan in the dark. I turn it on. Immediately there is a large boom. I have no idea what happened, but I have a sense that something is on the floor that should not be there. I look for the lights. When I turn them on, I see that a large bat must have been inside the fan. The bat has been cut in half by the blades of the fan. The pieces are lying on the floor. A bat. I thought I had landed in a country with some strange voodoo or something. A dead bat. That was my start in the Sudan."

He stayed awake, then went to his first practice at 5:30 in the morning. This was the normal practice time because of the summer heat. Practices would be done by 9:00 or 10:00 as the sun began to drain energy from the Khartoum population. The court, of course, was outdoors. There was one cramped indoor court in the city, but for some reason the national team never used it.

The program was run by the military. Feeley was driven everywhere by an army captain who apparently had little experience in driving. The truck bucked and bounced. The captain could never find reverse when needed. Feeley always asked if he could drive. The captain smiled. No English. There was an accident every few days as the captain drove the truck into trees or parked cars or whatever. Every practice started with a military formation. The players automatically stood in line according to height. Feeley rolled the leather balls he had brought from America onto the cement court. The games began. He gauged his talent.

"Here's the thing," he says, "these guys had watched highlight films of the NBA. Okay? So they went out and tried to do what the players in the NBA did. But no one had ever taught them how. They were a little bit off. It was like watching a film of someone playing golf and then going out to practice golf without ever having someone tell you what to do. I thought the level—this was the national team—was somewhere around Division II, college, in the States."

He heard rumors of a big player, but no one exceptionally tall was on the court. He taught basic drills, basic pieces of basketball fundamentals. Manute was in the south, home, spending time with his family. He was still mad about the events of the previous year. It wasn't until he heard a radio report that an American coach had arrived in Khartoum to work with the national team that he decided to come back. The trip took six days, walking combined with the ever-so-slow train from Wau. He arrived in time for one of the morning practices.

"This is the story that's always told," Feeley says. "The court was at the bottom of a hill. I come over the hill and look down. There's Manute. He's fixing the net on one of the baskets. He is just standing there, fixing the basket. I can't believe what I see. I ask one of the other players who this might be. He says, 'That's Manute. He's our friend. He plays on the team.' I say, 'Forget everything I've told you. We're changing the offense.' "

For some reason, the idea of Manute in America did not register. One plus one did not equal an immediate two. Feeley knew from the beginning that Manute was illiterate and did not know a word of English. What college could possibly take him? Feeley knew that Fairleigh Dickinson, for one, would not. He marveled at Manute simply as this undiscovered homegrown abnormality. Even the few English words Feeley would try to teach Manute were indecipherable when repeated because of the missing front teeth. Manute was simply Manute.

"He wanted to come to America, but they all wanted to come to America," Feeley says. "They had this vision of America from television or movies. They thought that all of America was 'Knots Landing.' What could I do? I figured Manute, because he was illiterate, didn't have a chance. They all had unrealistic expectations. I remember that Deng, who was very sharp, knew English very well, wanted me to talk to the pros. Well, Deng was a pretty good player, but the pros? Unrealistic."

A few scrimmages brought Feeley a touch of that unrealistic feeling himself. Maybe it was the heat. Maybe it was simply Manute. How good was he? Feeley had never seen anyone like him. Feeley's first thought was Bill Russell: Hadn't Russell won all those championships by blocking shots? Manute was a better shot blocker than Bill Russell ever was. Simple fact. He blocked shots that no one had ever blocked, jump shots from fifteen feet. The center who was supposed to be the lineal descendant of Russell in America was Patrick Ewing, the big kid from Cambridge, Massachusetts, who had gone along to Georgetown. Manute was better than Ewing. Wasn't he? Feeley had seen Ewing play. Maybe Ewing could do a lot more offensively. Manute could change a game more quickly on defense.

"All he had to do was stand away from a guy and wait," Feeley says. "He didn't even have to guard a guy close. He could just wait. The guy would have to come to him and the basket sometime. I had never seen anyone like him. On offense, he had instincts. You threw him the ball and he immediately looked the other way to make a pass. Instincts. He was a very good passer."

He still was only a summer project. No teeth. No English. No chance in the United States. Feeley ran the morning practices, then killed the rest of the hot day by hiring little kids to take him to points of interest in a city that had no points of interest. He ate peanuts, staying away from the fly-covered meat he saw hung in the marketplaces. Every now and then he ate pigeon, the bird served with the head attached, one eye looking at the diner throughout the meal. He did not try to make any crazy transatlantic phone calls about his discovery. He concentrated, instead, on another kid, Akila Shokai, who had been to the missionary schools and spoke fine English and was six feet nine. This seemed like a reasonable proposition.

"I think back now and Akila Shokai probably was one of the big reasons I was released from Fairleigh Dickinson," Feeley says. "I had it all set for him to come to school in September, start with the whole team, but things came up. He never cleared the country until January. I remember holding a big press conference at Fairleigh Dickinson in January and telling the reporters that a big man not only was coming from the Sudan to play for our team, but he was going to be in the lineup on Saturday. The president of the school read these quotes and didn't like them at all. He didn't like the image. He put a hold on everything. The kid's papers were fine, he was legitimate, but suddenly there had to be this big investigation. The kid eventually played four years at the school, but he never played a minute for me."

Feeley was fired at the end of the FDU season. His record for three years was 45–38, 17–12 in the final season.

*   *   *

"I never understood networking," Feeley says. "I look at it now and I should have been better at that. I guess I should have been nicer to Bobby Knight at Indiana or to someone famous. To have someone to call for me, to at least get me the interview to get the job. I just thought you won enough games and it happened. I never figured out the interviews. What are you supposed to say? I remember interviewing for the Georgetown athletic director's job before John Thompson was named coach. I asked, 'What about 1.6?' That was the requirement then that a player had to have a 1.6 grade average in high school to be admitted to college. They told me that the Ivy League was opposed for philosophical reasons and since they considered themselves like the Ivy League, they were also opposed. They would not honor it. Sure, except they were going to go under the 1.6 to find the players and they were going to try to keep the image. Sure. Georgetown is just like the Ivy League. Look at their teams. Sure. It's all so phony."

Feeley tried to figure out angles. What angle did he have that was different, that maybe would get him a job in this world he still could not figure? He remembered Manute. Maybe the tallest basketball player in the world would at least be the business card that would gain an interview. Take the tallest player in the world. Take me, too. A sort of finder's fee. He decided there were places that might take an illiterate basketball player who might, just might, be better than Patrick Ewing.

One of the first candidates to come to mind was Cleveland State, where Kevin Mackey was just starting work. Feeley knew Mackey a little bit from the time Mackey was an assistant at Boston College. Feeley knew Mackey was a coach who could "get things done." One of Mackey's stars at BC was John Bagley, a Bridgeport kid who supposedly had escaped high school with terrible grades. Another was Michael Adams of Hartford, more bad grades. Mackey could find ways to get kids into a relatively sophisticated school in Boston. What could he do in a smaller operation in Cleveland?

"Kevin always likes to act like he made great discoveries with Bagley and Adams," Feeley says. "Well, everybody knew who they were. They just couldn't figure out how to get them into school."

Feeley called with his proposition. He said he could deliver the tallest basketball player in the world from Africa if Mackey could deliver a scholarship for the player and another scholarship for Deng, the translator, and a job as assistant coach for Feeley. Mackey was interested. Feeley eventually found himself in May of 1983 at Logan Airport in Boston with Mackey and a man named Frank Catapano. They were waiting for a flight from Zurich that supposedly contained Manute and Deng.

"We had no idea if they were on the plane," Feeley says. "Mackey and this other guy—I figured he was the one who helped get things done—had sent the tickets. We didn't know anything after that. The plane was late. We were waiting and waiting. Finally, the plane arrived. We're standing outside customs and one of the first people out is Rick Pitino. Rick Pitino! He was the coach at Boston University then. He comes up to us and says, 'You won't believe what I saw on the plane! I saw the biggest man I've ever seen in my life!' Somehow Pitino doesn't put it all together. This was the strangest thing. Pitino doesn't figure it out. Kevin talks to him a little bit and he leaves."

An announcement came over the loudspeaker, a page for "Coach Don Feeley." Feeley responded. A customs agent was talking to Manute and Deng. The agent said Manute did not have any money at all, not a cent, and Deng claimed "Coach Don Feeley" would take responsibility. Was that the case?

"I'll take responsibility," Feeley said.

Manute was in America.

*　　*　　*

The attempt at a job failed. Mackey and Manute and Deng took a plane to Cleveland. Mackey told Feeley to go back to New Jersey and he would call in a few days. The few days passed. No call. A few more days passed. No call. Feeley called Mackey. What was the story? Mackey said he was all set for assistant coaches. Tough luck. Thank you for the tallest man in the world. What could Feeley do?

"I talked with Manute and Deng," he says. "I asked them if they were happy in Cleveland. They both said they were. I figured, let it go. If they were happy, fine. What Kevin did was not nice. What he did, he screwed me."

The only other approach Feeley tried was with the pros. He contacted Layden of the Utah Jazz, who had no interest. He contacted Lynam in San Diego with the Clippers. Lynam's pick of Manute, sight unseen, in the fifth round of the draft was promising. Maybe? Feeley flew to Cleveland to meet Lynam and watch Manute play. Lynam had an assistant's job open and, in fact, was also interviewing former Celtics guard Don Chaney for the position at dinner that night. Maybe? Feeley came prepared.

"First, we watch Manute," he says. "It was crazy. There was a scrimmage and all these players had shown up . . . but they showed up because they wanted to sell themselves. They're all playing like wild men because they know this coach of the San Diego Clippers is in the gym. No one would give Manute the ball. We're there just to watch Manute and he never sees the ball. I had to yell to Deng to start passing to him. All these guys were trying to make their own impressions."

Dinner followed. Feeley had developed some unconventional, simplistic approaches to basketball. His basic idea was that the best way to prepare to play basketball is to play basketball. Throw out all the playbooks, except maybe the ones that show how to move the ball in-bounds. Just play. Take the game of the playground, where everyone had learned to play anyway, and move it onto the gymnasium floor against all those boring, patterned operations. Run. Jump. Fly. Do what you have always done.

He had written down fifteen approaches to strategy that he thought were unique. All were simple when first stated, but deeper when considered for a moment. He laid them out, the work of a lifetime, on the dinner table. Chaney said nothing. Lynam nodded and worked into the dialogue. Feeley went through his list.

An example: "Number one: Don't get behind in a game. Isn't that the best way to win? Don't get behind. I was at a coaching clinic in Maine somewhere. Butch van Breda Kolff, who coached at Princeton with Bill Bradley on his team, was the speaker. He asked for questions. All of these guys from Maine were just sitting there, didn't have a thing to say. I hold up my hand. 'What would you do if there were ten seconds left, you're behind by one point and you have the ball?' I ask. Von Breda Kolff says that's simple, 'I'd give the ball to Bill Bradley.' 'All right,' I say. 'Perfect answer. But what do you do what you're behind by one point with ten minutes left and you have the ball? Why shouldn't you give the ball to Bill Bradley then, too? Why should the third-best, fourth-best kid be taking the shot? Play it the same way. Because *you don't want to get behind in the game.*"

Another example: "Look at the score to determine how you will play the rest of game. We had a game, when I was at Sacred Heart, when we trailed Bridgeport, 44–29, at the half. Write that down, 44–29. So I look at the score and say, 'All right, what are the most points we can probably score against this team in the second half if we start playing right?' I decided it was 50. That would be a good half for us, 50 points. Add that to the 29 we already have and what do you get? 79 points. That is the most we can get. Now, look at Bridgeport. How many points does Bridgeport have to score to reach 80 points to beat our 79? Bridgeport already has 44, so all it needs is 36 more points and it wins. So, while the obvious thing is that we need to score more in the second half, the really important thing is that we have to stop Bridgeport from scoring the 36. So what do we do? In this case we held the ball. Everyone thought we were crazy, but we held the ball. Final score? We win the game, 85–75."

Feeley talked and talked through the rest of his list. Lynam seemed interested. Chaney still said nothing. At the end of the meal, walking out the door, Lynam—according to Feeley, but denied by Lynam—pulled Feeley to one side.

"Don," Feeley says Lynam said. "I have to hire a black coach." Chaney was black. The job was gone. Manute was gone.

"I look back, I should have done something different," Feeley says. "I'm not exactly sure what, but it should have been different. I probably should have gone to [Howard] Garfinkel. Garfinkel knows everybody. He was mad I didn't go to him in the first place. Garfinkel would have figured something out."

Feeley is sitting now behind the wheel of his Dodge Caravan in a bank parking lot at a Glastonbury mall. The motor is running. This is March, the worst time to be out of a basketball job if you want a basketball job. Talk of the game is everywhere as teams have reached the round of sixteen in the NCAA. There has been snow in the morning. The parking lot is a mess. Handbags await.

"I ruined my first marriage because I was always out of the house because of basketball," he says. "Now, my second marriage, I'm never out of the house. It's funny how things work out. I get out of the house now to clean the yard. That's it. I don't know anybody where I live. I don't know anybody in the whole town. This is my wife's town."

He and his wife go to New York on business sometimes and he says she is always amazed at how he knows all of the little streets that no out-of-towner should know. This is because high schools and playgrounds and kids, players, were on these streets. What is the famous story about the college coach going into a bad neighborhood to find kids? It has been told so many times it must be true. The coach is looking for a particular high school and stops to ask a policeman for directions. The policeman says, "See that big building where someone was just pushed off the roof? That's the place you're looking for." A laugh. Has to be true.

The only coaching Feeley has done since Fairleigh Dickinson was a nine-month tour in Cairo as the coach of the Egyptian national team. He hated it. He hated Egypt. He hated the way the basketball was played, slow and deliberate, based on the European system. He hated the food. He hated the social system where a single, white, Christian man was unable to meet women, especially Muslim women. When he returned to the United States, he remarried and tried to become a golf pro for a while in Florida. That did not seem to work. He found that he did not even like golf very much. He moved north with his wife to work the handbag business.

"I'd like to be back in basketball," he says, "but I don't want to take a step backwards. So what do I do? I look at the jobs. What chance do I have at any of them? Everyone seems connected to everyone else. I guess . . . I guess I'm retired."

The motor runs. The van is in park. He mentions one particular Manute memory. A dinner was held at the University of Bridgeport a few years ago to retire Manute's number. Feeley sat at the head table when Manute gave his speech.

"I would like to thank Don Feeley, who was next to God," Manute said.

"What do you mean, next?" Feeley replied.

That was nice.

*And so it happened. The giant flew on an airplane
across much water. He drank diet soda and ate
peanuts that came from little packets of silver foil.
He watched a movie with little plugs in his ears.
He buckled his seat belt and landed in a place he
had only imagined.*

The Great Outside.

Here.

The visitor's name is Dale Robinson. He is black, six feet eight, obviously a player, a prospect at one time, but he is now twenty-eight years old. He is dressed in a long black leather coat and fills about half of Frank Catapano's tiny office in the basement of an accounting firm on Lewis Wharf in Boston. His head is near the ceiling. He is wearing a baseball cap on top of a face with a beatific grin. He has found the Lord.

"You can't see the wind, Frank," he is saying, "but you know it is there, don't you? You walk out on the street, you know there is a wind."

"I know there is a wind," Catapano says from behind his desk.

"You have a thought," Robinson continues. "You know you have a thought, but you can't see it. You're having a thought right now, even though you can't see it. Aren't you?"

"I know I am having a thought, Dale."

"Then why can't you know there is a God? Even if you can't see God, can't you know He is there? Why is the existence of God so much harder to accept than the existence of the wind or a thought?"

Robinson's conversion came in the past year, after nine bullets were pumped into his body in a shooting he calls "a case of mistaken identity." He survived the wounds and he found God. Robinson says, to tell the truth, he always believed in God, even when he was doing the drugs and running the streets and squandering assorted chances at assorted junior colleges. The shooting was a sign he should put his belief to work. The shooting put his life in focus. He is now a street minister. He is back in school at tiny Bunker Hill Community College, even playing some basketball again. He is a terror on the community college circuit.

"He's turned his life around," Catapano says. "It's been something to see. He's gone 180 degrees in the past year. I don't know about all of this religion, but if it works, then that's good enough for me. You can't believe the change in Dale. He was wild. He was as wild as they come. You couldn't tell him anything."

"I'm averaging 28–30 points a game," Robinson says. "Getting some rebounds. Doing everything."

"What do you mean *you're* averaging 28–30 points a game? Where's the Lord in this? I thought *He* was the most important factor in everything."

"What I mean," Robinson says, "is that He is averaging 28–30 points a game, through me. I am His instrument. Can't you see that? He is working through me. He is even telling me to pass the ball more."

Catapano is Manute's agent. Catapano is also Robinson's agent, though "friend" might be a better term because no money is involved and there are no teams bidding for Robinson's services and certainly never will be. Catapano is agent to a collection of basketball characters that would fill out any Fox Network sit-com. His wife tells him he is the lead character in the Woody Allen movie *Broadway Danny Rose*. Catapano says he has no sword-swallowers, no fire-eaters, no jugglers, but his wife probably is right. He is Manute's agent, which is a definite start. He is the agent for Michael Adams and Scott Brooks, two of the smallest players in the NBA. He is the agent for John Bagley, the pudgy point guard of the Celtics. He is the agent for a succession of low-budget basketball players strung across the minor leagues and Europe. He also is half owner of a pizza place, which is run by his brother-in-law.

"How many agents can negotiate a contract, then take the client back to his restaurant and cook him a good pizza?" he says. "You have to say that's different."

He is fifty years old, way overweight, going on a diet as soon as he finishes this bagel here, and never really intended to be in the agent business. It all somehow evolved. He liked basketball, always did, as a kid in Great Neck, New York. He was the manager of the basketball team when he went to Boston College as an undergraduate, not just a collector of towels, but a manager who scrimmaged with the team. He stuck around the school for law school, then stayed in Boston as a young lawyer. He always liked the basketball.

"My first business is real estate," he says. "Nobody knows that, but it's true. I'm involved with some older buildings, small buildings that contain 7-Eleven's, places like that. Collect the rent. Pay the mortgage. That's the foundation. The agent business . . . with the money that's involved now in pro basketball, it certainly can be lucrative, but I don't know how much I can do in it. Do you know that there are over four hundred agents registered with the NBA Players' Association? There are only 350 players, tops, if you figure twelve players for every team, plus maybe twenty-five more on injured reserve. What do all these agents do? I don't have any superstars, but I have seven players in the league. How many of these guys don't even have a player? I counted it up the other day. There are 102 agents who have players and a lot of them have only one. How much competition does that make? How do you get a player? I don't know how it's done anymore. Do you have to go in there with all kinds of flash and promises? I can't do that. I'm always wondering how long I'm going to be in this business."

He became a founding member of a basketball booster club at Boston College. That was a start. How could he help the program? He was not only a fan, he was an aggressive fan. He remembers being at a meeting, a cocktail party, where he was introduced to a new assistant coach, Kevin Mackey. The introduction was "Frank, as the man who wants to see Boston College go into the big time more than anyone else I know, meet Kevin, the coach who wants to see Boston College go into the big time more than any coach I know." The friendship was immediate. Catapano was soon riding with Mackey around New England, going to high school games, talking to coaches, meeting kids.

The two explorers would travel to the worst ghettos in Bridgeport, Hartford, New Haven, down into Harlem, hard urban landscapes where they would keep the car locked until a door opened in a grim project building and some kid would walk across the cracked concrete. This sometimes seemed to be a rescue mission as well as recruiting. Catapano called Mackey "sort of a Jack Kerouac of basketball." They would watch summer games in playgrounds, the only white men on the scene. They would search for that elusive talent, the kid buried under so much neglect that no one else knew he existed. They succeeded.

"One night Kevin calls me from Hartford," Catapano says. "It must have been twelve-thirty, one o'clock. I was asleep. I thought something terrible must have happened. He's all excited. He says, 'Frank, I'm in this phone booth and my palms are sweating. That's how good this kid is. My palms are sweating.' The kid was Michael Adams."

A bond developed, Catapano and Mackey tied together by their insider knowledge. It was like traveling through an urban version of the antique shops and flea markets of New England, looking for that rare piece of glassware or the painting that no one else recognized as valuable. The gem. Let the self-proclaimed experts and geniuses go to the showrooms and deliver their opinions. This was backroads-discovery stuff on earthier, more exciting turf. Your own eyes made the decisions. You made your own call. Player? Or not? To find a gem—a Bagley or an Adams—and then to foist it on the world was the greatest kick. *How much did you pay for that? Oh, I got it at a yard sale.* That was the fun. To confound the geniuses.

"I'm always wary of experts," Catapano says. "I'm wary of the basketball geniuses. What makes a genius? I think I can look at a player and tell whether or not he can play. I can't tell whether or not he will succeed, because there are things inside that a player has to have, a desire to succeed, that no one can see right away. But I can tell if he has a chance.

"The geniuses? I don't know. I used to argue about the geniuses a lot more when I was younger. Who makes them geniuses? Like Red Auerbach. The genius. I met him once in my life. I was with Larry Fleischer. We were at the Big East tournament at Madison Square Garden. Red sat behind us. This is what I heard him say . . . most of the time he seemed to be sleeping during the games. His eyes were closed, anyway. He woke up once and Sherman Douglas of Syracuse drove to the basket and scored. Red said, 'That kid's a good player,' and he was right. Sherman Douglas was a good player. Red went back to sleep, then woke up again when Dana Barros of BC drove and scored. Red said, 'That kid's quick,' and he was right again. Dana Barros was quick. That's all I heard during the entire game. Two things. Both of them were right. I used to argue about Red, but I guess he is a genius, after all. Both things I ever heard him say were right."

The BC association led Catapano into the agent business. He

was always around the program, following the kids he and Mackey had found. That was the fun. Watching them blossom. Bagley, the backcourt gem found in Bridgeport, youngest of seventeen kids, a spectacular college player and a serviceable pro, was his first client. Catapano wasn't even looking for the business. He helped the late Fleischer, a big-name agent, a friend, secure Bagley. Fleischer suggested Catapano be a co-agent. That seemed like more fun. Profitable fun. Bagley led to another client, to another and another and, well, to Manute.

"Kevin had become head coach at Cleveland State," Catapano says. "We were still friends. He was trying to put the thing together. He'd call and we'd talk about all sorts of things. I was active with the AAU team here. We'd talk about kids. He was looking for kids from here because he knew all the high school coaches, all the people involved. One day, he calls and tells me he can get this seven-foot-seven guy from the Sudan. Would I like to be involved in bringing him over here? I ask if he's got a picture. The history with these African guys is that they're always about five inches shorter than they're supposed to be. He says he's got a picture. He says the picture is unbelievable. I'm intrigued."

Why not? Talk about the ultimate flea market story. This had a chance to be the greatest scam of them all, the biggest find. Big? Seven-seven. Mackey was bringing the players—Manute and Deng—from Khartoum on a recruiting visit. Totally legal under NCAA rules. Cleveland State was paying for the airline tickets. The rules said a recruit must return home in forty-eight hours from his visit, using his return ticket, but what if the recruit didn't return? What if he didn't want to return? What if there were political problems or something else that made him afraid to return? Perfect. Mackey was cutting Catapano in on the action. Catapano was bringing in a few bucks.

"Not a lot of money," he says. "Not much at all. The NCAA

got it all wrong later on. They made it sound like much more. It was about a tenth of what the NCAA had in its report. I didn't think I was doing anything wrong. I certainly wasn't doing anything that was illegal, according to the law. The NCAA laws? That was Kevin's responsibility. If anything was wrong, he would be accountable. It's different now, the NCAA certification of agents has penalties to the agent for infractions, but there wasn't anything like that then. I figured Kevin knew what was right and wrong."

The idea that money could be made, somewhere in the future, was only a hazy, back-of-the-mind, lottery sort of thought. Who could predict? This was a low-budget shot on the wildest of stock tips. Feeley was the only one who had actually seen Manute play. In Africa. Against Africans. Who knew if Manute could play top-level college ball? Any ball? Catapano and Mackey didn't even know Feeley very well. Catapano, in fact, didn't know him at all. Maybe Mackey could dream of a big payoff involving an NCAA championship and one of those job-for-life contract deals that a Dean Smith has at North Carolina, fame and fortune and knowing the color commentators on a first-name basis. He would be the coach, with immediate contact with Manute, with the immediate benefits if there were any. Everything was more murky with Catapano. What were his benefits? That four years later, after this guy proved to be the greatest player in the history of the world, he would need an agent and would stick with the first agent he ever saw? That the guy would make billions and 10 percent of the billions would be wonderful? Seriously, what were the chances of that?

The lottery image was best. But the ticket. Enjoy the excitement of the big wheel turning around. Enjoy the excitement of the airport, waiting for the plane to land. What's the financial cost? The payment for a few extra English lessons? Maybe the payment of some hotel bills? Spin the wheel. This was not an investment in some blue-chip moneymaker. This was a chip put on green felt, nothing more. The big rush.

"Tell me this, who was being hurt?" Catapano says. "Was Manute being illegally recruited away from anyone else? No one else wanted him. No one else knew about him. Was Manute being hurt? He was the one who wanted to come. This was helping him. This was a deal that helped everyone involved. It was the experience of a lifetime. I was never involved with anything like it before and I will never be involved in anything like it again.

"You should have seen Kevin and me at the airport. We were like a pair of two-year-olds, we were so excited. Then, when Pitino came off that plane, it was only better. Then Manute . . . I remember he was wearing this tan leisure suit."

The delay in the arrival of the plane from Zurich meant that now there was a layover of perhaps six hours in Boston before the next plane left for Cleveland with Mackey and Feeley and the two players. Why stay around the airport? Catapano took everybody into Boston for a meal at his pizza place. This was Manute's first look at America. He was squeezed into the back of Catapano's car. A tunnel takes travelers into the city on the short trip from the airport. The tunnel was filled with late-afternoon commuters, horns and congestion, cars everywhere.

"Where's everybody going?" Manute asked in Dinka.

"They're going home from work," Deng said.

"All these people?" Manute asked. "Why do they have to be rushing all over the place?"

Dinner was served at Mike's Pizza, named after Catapano's brother-in-law and located along the Freedom Trail, a string of red bricks that connects Paul Revere's House and the Old North Church and the burial site of Mother Goose and other attractions for the Boston tourist. Catapano then took everyone to Matignon High School in Cambridge, where he had to pick up his daughter. She suggested the group go to Catapano's house in the suburbs. There was time.

"My son, I guess he was about eleven, was playing basketball in the driveway with another kid when we pulled up," Catapano says. "Manute gets out of the car and keeps on getting. You should have seen my son's eyes. That was worth it, right there."

Catapano served everybody orange juice. Manute looked at the furnishings in the house. He was fascinated by the grand piano in the living room, sitting at the seat, playing with the keys. There were a lot of questions, through Deng, about the NBA. There were answers. The orange juice was finished, everyone went back to the car, out to the airport. The NCAA later made a big deal of the entire six-hour interval, declaring it all illegal entertainment of a recruit. Catapano says he considers it only hospitality.

He did not see Manute again for eight months, until Washington's Birthday weekend, when he visited Cleveland with his wife. He did not see Manute after that until the summer, when Manute came to Boston. Catapano stretched out two mattresses, end to end, in the basement. A short visit by a long man. There was a memorable three-on-three in the driveway, Catapano and his three sons and a neighbor and Manute. Catapano remembers Manute, stretched across two couches, cheering as an athlete from the Sudan won a medal for pistol shooting in the Olympics on television. The effects of the English lessons were obvious. Manute was more natural, ready to talk. Catapano saw that from the moment they arrived at the house.

"Manute," he said, preparing to unlock the door. "This is a key . . ."

"Frank," Manute said. "Don't you think we have keys in Khartoum?"

Catapano says he will never become involved with an athlete from Africa again. This gamble surely has turned out fine because he has been Manute's agent all the way and made some money, but the time spent has been out of proportion. He, alone, has been a part of Manute's life since the big man arrived in

Boston. He has been a sounding board, a solver of problems—and there have been many. He has grown to know the procedures of the U.S. Immigration Office very well.

"Here's the wildest day I ever spent in my life," he says. "Manute had to leave the country and reenter to renew his visa. It didn't make sense to go back to the Sudan to do it, so we went to Nassau. I fly out of Boston at four o'clock in the morning to meet Manute in Washington. We take a plane to Atlanta, then to Miami, then to Nassau. We're walking to the passport office in Nassau and everybody, of course, just stops and stares at Manute. Four Rastafarians—with the dreadlocks?—start giving him a hard time. They're asking how tall he is, the whole bit. They start touching him. Manute gets mad. He starts fighting with the Rastafarians. It's a scene. I get him away, we get the visa, back on the plane. Miami. Raleigh-Durham. Washington. Back to Boston.

"I don't have the time anymore to devote to one client like that. I have a family. I would have done Manute that one time for the hell of it. I wouldn't do another guy from Africa for the hell of it. Somewhere you have to make money. I made money with Manute, but it took a lot of time. Don't get me wrong. I wouldn't trade the time with Manute for anything. I just don't have that kind of time now."

The NCAA later determined that Catapano had provided "at least $6,100" to Manute and Deng during one year at Cleveland State. Catapano says the figure certainly was "less than $5,000." He points out that Manute and Deng certainly did not live "in the lap of luxury" in their first year. There was no car. There were no luxuries. The two players led a subsistence-level existence—if that. What did he do wrong? He says he did nothing. He helped two people. He helped himself, perhaps, in the long run, but he also helped two people. What's wrong with that?

"I suppose, if I learned anything here, it's that you're better off doing everything by the book," Catapano says. "If I ever did it again, I'd do it by the book. In life, though, it's hard to do everything by the book. You know? Even the person with the greatest morals ever, it's hard to do everything by the book. You see some real sad things out there."

He has become something of a middle-aged philosopher. He quotes lines from movies, from books. You know what bothers him most? Boring people. He does not have time for the social flimflam, the average conversation. Why waste time? He would rather be talking with characters, with people a few steps away from the norm. The agent business is good for that. He is on the phone with his players in Europe, his players in the CBA, his cast of characters. Did you know he had a player even taller than Manute? He did. The guy's name was George Bell. He was seven-nine.

"He lived down around Raleigh-Durham," Catapano says. "He was working in a warehouse somewhere. Had been out of school for a while. He called me, I guess, because he heard that I was Manute's agent. I got him a tryout with the L.A. Clippers. He wasn't bad, but he had no stamina. Up and down the court and he was done. He couldn't cut it. That's Manute's strength. He has a great heart. He's aggressive. He wants to succeed. George Bell? I don't know where he is now. I heard he was working sometimes at trade shows as The World's Tallest Man. Nice guy. He just couldn't cut it."

The character for this day seems to be Robinson, the born-again street minister and community college jump shooter with the bullet wounds in his stomach. Robinson appears to be a frequent visitor in the little office, talking with Catapano about basketball and life and life, of course, after death. Catapano is the cynic in the conversation, the devil's advocate, questioning everything Robinson says. Robinson is the True Believer. There is a pleasant rhythm to the words.

"Do you still have that book I gave you?" Robinson asks. "Or did you throw it away?"

"I have it right here," Catapano says, rummaging through some papers to find a blue paperback copy of the New Testament. "I'm going to read it, too. I've read some already."

"You're keeping it hidden in those papers, Frank. Take it out."

Catapano puts the New Testament on top of the papers. See? He will have it at hand when needed. Robinson nods at the new position. This is where the book should be. On top.

"Dale could have been good," Catapano says. "He could have been a first-round draft choice. He could have been another Malik Sealy."

"Malik who?" Robinson asks. "Who are you talking about?"

"Malik Sealy. He's going to be a first-round draft choice from St. John's."

"Huh. St. John's. I wouldn't have been any Malik. Air Jordan. That's who I would have been. Air Dale."

Catapano looks across his desk at his reborn client. Let the other agents go for the boring. The buzz of commerce doesn't have to be a flat line across a screen. Do something you want to do. Take chances. Have a little fun. Life is too short. Isn't that the commercial? Something like that. Air Jordan? Air Dale?

"Air head," Catapano says in a nice way. "That would be more like it."

The giant lived first in Cleveland. Cleveland? The tricks he could do with the round ball were greatly appreciated. He learned to talk a new language and live a new sort of life. A different life. He was lonely sometimes, so far from home, but he made new friends. He learned.

In Cleveland.

This is the first week of April 1991. The color in Kevin Mackey's face is not good. He has a gray, indoors look. He is in his ninth month of sobriety, heading for number ten, and this has been a fight. His face is the evidence. His life has turned sour and the process happened in full public view. He is working back in anonymity. The work is hard. Very hard.

He is living in an apartment in Houston and working every day at the John Lucas New Spirit Treatment and Recovery Center. He is trying to rehabilitate his name as much as anything. Who wants a coach who has been arrested coming out of a crack house at 7:30 on a Friday night? The old job at Cleveland State is gone. The family in Chagrin Falls, a Cleveland suburb, is pretty much gone. Some friends have stuck with him and some have not. He has to work through his problems on his own. He is a self-proclaimed recovering alcoholic.

"I've been in a bar twice in nine months," he says. "Both times it was with guys from the clinic to watch sports events on television. We sat in a corner, drank Diet Cokes, watched the events and left."

He is forty-four years old and only five years ago he was proclaimed in the Cleveland newspapers as "the King of Cleveland." He took a team of unpedigreed nobodies into the NCAA tournament, upset Indiana, and lost by only a point on a disputed call to David Robinson and Navy in the Sweet Sixteen. He created interest where none ever existed, finding kids nobody else wanted—or nobody else could touch academically—and making them into winners. He bent all the rules he could bend and some of the rules he couldn't. He was a coaching skyrocket, a fast-talking Irishman from Boston, funny and quotable and bright, a self-admitted basketball confidence man. He threw out the first pitch of the Cleveland Indians' 1986 baseball season, heard the cheers of a filled Municipal Stadium.

The skyrocket has landed now. He has a desk in the hallway of the Lucas Center. People exit the elevator at the second floor and find Mackey, usually drinking a Diet Coke. He is the first coach to be enrolled in the program. He had been rooming and working with Chris Washburn, a onetime number one draft choice of the Golden State Warriors who had succumbed to the lure of crack cocaine. Washburn, alas, has succumbed again and left in the last week. He was seen on a street corner a few days earlier, wired, mumbling about snakes. Mackey is moving along, working with whatever players arrive with their problems. The latest is Roy Tarpley, the former first-round pick of the Dallas Mavericks. Tarpley, whose past problem was cocaine, has been arrested again and checked himself into the program. This is a drug clinic for the basketball famous.

"If you just sat where I sit every day, you'd have some stories," Mackey says. "The people who come here . . . you'd be very surprised at some of the names. Sitting here would be like having a tape recorder in the confessional. You'd have some very good stories."

There is a light in his eyes at that remark. A tape recorder in the confessional. Yes, that would be something. Wouldn't it? A hustler's dream. The eyes show the music is still inside the rehabilitating Kevin Mackey somewhere.

"I'm addicted to basketball more than anything else," he says. "I've always said the game grabs you when you're a kid and doesn't let you go. That's me. I was never the best player, a real ham-and-egger as a matter of fact, but I was always the most enthusiastic. I was the kid who conned all the other kids into shoveling off the court in the winter. I was the organizer."

He grew up in Somerville, Massachusetts, a working-class suburb tucked beside Boston and Cambridge. When he was a kid, Somerville was mad for basketball, the home of the best and most feared high school team in the state. The Eastern Massachusetts and New England tournaments were held at the nearby Boston Garden and the residents of the town would walk, en masse, to see the local teenagers play on the same parquet floor where Cousy and Russell and the Celtics won championships. The building would be filled, 13,909 spectators gathered to watch one school or another, but the Somerville people would dominate. The traditional Somerville spot was the second balcony. Kids brought large piles of newspapers, which were torn to make confetti. Somerville would come onto the floor to the strains of "Somerville Leads the Way" and the Garden would be filled with a newspaper blizzard. Was there anything more exciting? If the unthinkable happened—Somerville lost and was eliminated—the walk home would become a moving riot, store windows broken, cars overturned.

Mackey watched all this and never forgot. He didn't go to Somerville, wasn't big enough to play at the high school, playing instead at smaller St. Polycarp's High in Cambridge. He also played on the CYO circuit and in the local YMCAs. The image of Somerville still grabbed him. He was hooked, a short man in fatal love with a big man's game. He went to St. Anselm's College in Burlington, Vermont, sat on the bench, then started looking for his first coaching job. Hooked.

"He was a born coach," says younger brother, Joe, now a Boston lawyer and state representative. "He was a coach at home for me when we were kids. When I was about thirteen years old, scoring 30 points in junior high school, he told me to give up basketball and stick to baseball, which I also played. I'll never forget it. 'Joe,' he said, 'you are not a basketball player. There are kids whose elbows grow inside. Those are the kids who are made for basketball. Your elbows grow outside. Kids whose elbows grow outside are made for baseball. Billy Endicott is the basketball player from your team. His elbows grow inside.' I thought he was crazy at the time, but he was absolutely right. I turned out to be a far better baseball player than basketball player. Billy Endicott turned out to be a great basketball player."

Mackey's first coaching job was at Cathedral High, a small and struggling parochial school in Boston's South End. The school was mostly white but located in the middle of black housing projects. Mackey had already determined that black players (presumably black players whose elbows grow inside) win championships. He went immediately to the nun who was the principal of the school and told her it was time the school did something for the community in which it was located. Did the school want to be a white island in the midst of a black environment?

"What do you have in mind, Kevin?" the nun asked.

"I think about fifteen minority scholarships would be fine, Sister," Mackey replied.

He was on his way.

After a couple of years at Cathedral, he moved along to Don Bosco, a bigger high school, bigger program. Now he could recruit the entire city. He patrolled the Roxbury ghetto, was a well-known figure in the projects, always driving a big American car, a Lincoln or a Cadillac, a "big ride" that attracted the players. They liked to play with the automatic windows, turn the knobs on the stereo. He was always talking, always looking for an edge. He built a state champion that was as good as any of the Somerville champions. His teams were filled with tough, impoverished kids who went to school and stayed in school. He made sure. The kids were his magic beans, planted in the ground. He treated them well, forcing them to study, preparing them for college as best he could. He wanted them to grow and flower. He wanted to grow with them, developing his ideas of a pressing defense and a running offense, blitzkrieg basketball. He was also not averse to a good dose of that familiar standby—height.

"When I was a coach in high school, I had a rule that any kid over six feet made the freshman team," he says. "I didn't care how the kid played. Who knows at that age? All kids develop different. Some of the best ones, ever, were late bloomers. Michael Jordan was cut from his high school team. Who knows?

"When I took the job at Don Bosco, I asked the principal if there were any kids in the school who were tall. He said there was a six-foot-seven freshman named Joe Beaulieu, but they were throwing the kid out. He never came to school. Never came. I called the kid's mother. She was having problems. The father was gone. The kid just didn't want to go to school. She didn't know what to do with him. I asked her if I could help. I said if she could convince the kid to repeat the year, I would help him stay in school. I said I would make sure he got to school every day. I would call him every morning to make sure he was up and he was coming. The woman was very relieved. I called the kid every day. When he was a senior, he was the player of the year, we were state champions, and I was coach of the year. The kid was accepted at Harvard. . . ."

The schemes were always cooking. Something was always happening. Mackey tells the story about himself with Patrick Ewing. How far would Mackey go? Ewing was in the eighth grade, already six feet nine and known to half the college coaches in

America. The familiar, cultivated American daydream. Mackey was coaching a summer clinic. Ewing appeared, wearing a pair of older but certainly serviceable sneakers. Mackey approached him and asked about the shoes. Didn't Ewing know that wearing a pair of old sneakers could possibly result in injury? Wasn't Ewing worried about that? You know, the players at Don Bosco received a pair of brand new sneakers every season. At *Don Bosco. New sneakers.*

"The next day Ewing comes to the clinic and he's wearing new sneakers," Mackey says. "He said he went home and told his father what I'd said about getting hurt in old sneakers and his father took him right out to the store. Terrible, huh? Here's a guy, how much extra money did he have? Buying the kid sneakers because of what I'd said. Terrible. I felt like I was about a foot high."

The high school successes took him to Boston College, Division I, for an assistant's job under Dr. Tom Davis. Mackey became the dark assistant that every college basketball team has, the recruiter, the dealer, the conniver on the edge of the rules. Dr. Tom would take the talent and diagram the plays and talk to the press with the detached demeanor of an official White House spokesman. Mackey would do the menial tasks. He would drive through the night with Catapano or whomever was with him, go by himself, take the big ride into the streets and bring home the talent in body bags. Bagley. Adams. An English kid named Martin Clark, who lived in Boston. A line of kids. Good players. Great players, some of them. BC had basketball success it never had.

"The big thing in recruiting is finding out who has the kid's ear," Mackey says. "That's the key. A lot of people will think they know someone who has the kid's ear, but it may be someone entirely different. You have to find out who. Everyone may think it's the mother who will have the word, but maybe it's a pimp on the street corner. You have to find out. You have to recruit the pimp if he's going to determine where the kid goes."

Davis left BC in 1982. Mackey applied for the head job but didn't get it. The school was afraid of him, not so afraid of the things he had done as an assistant in the background, but afraid of him in the front of the program. He stayed for a year with new coach Gary Williams, but was always looking for an opportunity. Cleveland State, an obscure outpost on the Division I map, finally called. Mackey jumped. The wise minds in Boston predicted he would either wind up with a national championship or with the school on probation forever. Even money. Actually, he almost did both. He almost won the national championship. The school wound up on probation.

Enter Manute. He was the player who probably could have finalized the national championship. He was also the player who was the reason for the probation. All of the above. A tidy story.

The typical Mackey recruit at Cleveland State was the same recruit Mackey had found for BC—the same recruit he had found for his Boston high schools, except now the kid was four years older and without the guidance of a Mackey figure through high school. These were kids with problem grades and problem lives from East Coast problem neighborhoods, leftover kids. Yet even with their problems, if they had been a little taller or a little wider or a little more controllable, a little something, they would have been scooped up by more famous schools. They were mostly a couple inches too short, a couple of credits shy, a couple of something less than what the big schools desired. Mackey was waiting. He ran a last-chance hotel.

"I like the type of player who gets right up on you, who bothers you," Mackey says. "I like the kid you hate to play against. Do you know what I mean? There are a lot of players, players in the NBA, Kenny Smith right here in Houston is an example, excellent players, hit the jump shot, run the break, but they don't bother you when you play. I want the kid who bothers you. The aggressive, mean kid. The kid with the aggressive streak. Unfortunately, most of those kids come from dysfunctional families, bad situations. That is where you have to look. I always said that if I were the golf coach, you would have found me prowling the country clubs. I'm not the golf coach. I went where the players were."

He immediately built a team that featured speed and scoring with these tough, undersized kids looking for a chance. He called his approach to the game "run and stun," ten kids playing in every game, creating full-court, fast-break mayhem. It was an exciting game to watch, an exciting game to play, a successful game on the back-road Whatever Conference schedule Cleveland State was playing. The Mid-Continent Conference. There was only one weak spot in the operation, one limit on how far the team could go. What was the most important piece on the X and O blackboard? What was missing? There was no Joe Beaulieau, already enrolled, just waiting at the school to be the team's big man. The big man, known by everybody, recruited by everybody, cultivated even in the worst circumstances, was the player Mackey could not find. The big men had all been found already.

Hadn't they?

The call from Feeley was a revelation. Of course. A big man from Africa. What could be better? The ultimate player from the ultimate ghetto. Everything merged together neatly in Mackey's mind. He didn't have to be convinced, cajoled, or persuaded in any way. Mind and subject were a perfect dreamlike match. He brought Catapano into the action. This brought Manute and Deng into the country on their forty-eight-hour recruiting visit that would ultimately never end. What could be better? The sighting of Pitino at Logan Airport was the biggest laugh of all. Mackey took the biggest basketball player imaginable, stashed him in a hotel and then a dormitory in Cleveland, and tried to figure out what to do next. Did he have the all-time recruiting secret or what? Forget the fact that Manute could not read or speak a word of English. Look at him. Look.

"I knew it was going to be hard," Mackey says. "I went to the president of the university. He had told me, when I first came, that he would try to help. I said, 'Look, I've never asked you for anything. This is one time. Can you give me a little help?' He looked at the situation. He said he just couldn't do it."

Deng was fine. He was fluent in English, had grades, had a diploma. His basketball wasn't good enough for Division I standards, but Mackey gave him a scholarship as the Cleveland State manager. Manute was the project. How could he learn English in a flash? How could he become eligible? Mackey roomed him with Deng, then went searching for an English as second language program. He found it at nearby Case Western Reserve University.

"They showed up, Mackey and Manute and Deng and maybe an assistant coach," Arleen Bialic, now the director of the Case program, says. "It was amazing. This was like the end of May, maybe early June. They said they wanted Manute to learn English by September. I looked at the situation. I had never been involved with anyone like this. I eventually wound up writing a professional paper about it. He was starting from ground zero, not only in English, but in twentieth-century culture. He had no cultural awareness at all. He couldn't use a telephone. He couldn't operate a Coke machine. He didn't even know how to hold a pencil, never had done it. I said, 'Learn English by September? You'll be lucky if he's learned to use the bathroom by September.'"

The lessons began anyway. Someone would drive Manute to Bialic's office every weekday morning. For three hours, she and Manute would take baby steps into this new language. She knew no Dinka and little Arabic. She said Manute knew mostly a basic, market Arabic. Manute's first pencil was one of those fat children's pencils, flat on the sides, easy to grip. The first words were learned from pictures in magazines. Basketball magazines. Any magazines.

"What is this man doing?" Bialic would ask, holding a picture of a swimmer. "He is swim-ming."

"Swim-ming," Manute would reply.

The money for the lessons was paid, up front, mostly in cash or money orders. The lessons went slowly. Bialic found Manute to be intelligent, with a good sense of humor. He would become excited when he saw pictures of things he knew. He liked cars. He liked the typewriter, sitting over it and figuring out the keys and making words. He liked to look at the pictures of cows.

"He loved cows for some reason," Bialic says. "He'd say that our cows weren't like their cows, but he'd look at the markings. Cows. He loved cows."

Bialic sometimes would bring him lunch. He did not like much American food. He liked peanut butter. He liked pizza. Sometimes Bialic would take him out to lunch. Cars would literally stop. People would stare. She had the distinct feeling that this experiment was supposed to be kept under wraps. There were no stories about Manute in the newspaper. Everything seemed to be couched in secrecy. She learned that Manute had been told not to ride the bus. She presumed it was part of the secrecy, but found it was also because the Cleveland State coaches were worried, something about Cleveland street kids wanting to "take down this biggest bird of prey." She felt more than a bit sorry for Manute, completely isolated from his environment, a situation, she says, that can be "very, very debilitating."

"It was a completely unique situation," Bialic says. "You just don't find people like that. There was never one like Manute before he came, there has never been one since. There never will be. The people you teach, who come here, are usually literate in some other language that you can relate to. Mongolians. We have Mongolians here now, but they have this other language. Manute . . . his culture had no written word. He had no experience with it. It is easier to teach a child to learn English, because you have time, because the child is growing into the culture as he is growing into the language. Manute? He was very bright, but he had to learn the culture as fast as he had to learn the language."

In the early days, Manute sometimes became lonely and depressed. Would he ever learn? He would get homesick and think that maybe all of this was not a very good idea. Deng would talk to him, keep him going.

"You're in America, as people say, 'the land of opportunity,' " Deng would say. "You're seven feet seven. You're going to be the tallest player in the United States if you go to college, and if you go to the NBA you'll be the tallest player there. So stick to the English. I'll help you out. You've got to sweat it out. Your future is in the United States. If you go back to the Sudan, there's nothing for you there."

Manute would nod and keep going.

The easiest place to adjust to this new country, this new life, was the basketball court. If Manute had problems with other areas, basketball was a universal language. Height translates to height. He had arrived in the off-season, so his first basketball was played in pickup games at Cleveland State's old Woodling Gymnasium. These were grand pickup games, filled with Cleveland State players and local NBA players from the Cavaliers and other teams. Anyone who was looking for high-level action. If Manute was not ready for conversation at the Algonquin roundtable, he was still ready for basketball with NBA players like Charles Oakley and Ron Harper and Alvin Robertson and Mark West and Brad Sellers and Bagley. There were no primer lessons. He walked onto the court. He fit. He more than fit.

"Coach Mackey had told me that someone was coming," Sean Hood, a Cleveland State player, now an assistant coach at the school, says. "He said, 'I've got a special treat coming for you.'

When I saw Manute, I couldn't believe it. He was unbelievable. All I saw was W's on the schedule. How could we lose? I'm still convinced, if Manute ever played with our team that beat Indiana, we never would have lost a game."

It took a while to figure him out. That was the first basketball lesson about Manute. How do you play against this guy? Normal shots, normal moves, did not work. Take the ball to the basket? Not against Manute. He blocked shot after shot. The idea seemed to be that the shot had to be taken beyond a ten-foot radius around Manute or directly in front of his face, so his arms could not move in close. The idea took a while to develop and even then it did not always work. Manute blocked shots no one had ever blocked before.

The players called him "The Warrior." Manute called the players by various names or by the all-purpose name Dude. What was it they said? He didn't know English, but he sure liked to talk. He quickly used all the phrases of the practice game, saying, "Let's get busy," or "I'm kicking it," or "My bad." No introductions were necessary. None of the American black kids had ever really known an African, and Manute had surely never known American black kids, but there was an easy, natural bond. A connection. Manute used the word *homeboy*. Hey, homeboy. Brother. He fit the environment, another first-generation black kid in this new experience of college, even if he wasn't officially enrolled or maybe even a kid. Another basketball player. He became angry at the basketball times when anger was appropriate, throwing a ball at someone after an elbow, holding his hands up to fight. Hell, he fought. He fought anyone. There was never the feeling that he was a second-class visitor from any second-class country. Seven feet seven. The Warrior. Mess with him and he'd kick your ass. He fought and he laughed at the right places and he fit. Deng was around to help with the translation of all curses, jokes, or observations. The cultural gulf the English teacher saw was never seen by the players. When he became tired at the fast pace of the game, skinny as he was, he simply sat.

"Manute is on vacation," he said.

The players laughed. He laughed.

"You know what?" Hood says. "From the first day, I don't think Manute was ever in awe of America. It was America that was in awe of Manute."

He made friends. He and Deng soon moved from the Holiday Inn, where they first had landed, to the In Town Apartments, where all the other players lived. A freshman named Warren Bradley from Bridgeport, Connecticut, was their third roommate for a couple of weeks. Still their friend after he moved to a two-man room, he would often go back to the Africans' room, always noticing a smell of curry and garlic. The players would all hang around together. They would explore.

"Deng was mostly all business," Bradley says. "Very intelligent. Very responsible, sort of Manute's overseer. Manute was also intelligent, but more social. He always wanted to be doing something. He'd say, 'Let's take a walk,' 'Let's go someplace.' I wound up with him a lot more than with Deng. He was very arrogant, very proud. That's how I would describe him. I sort of envied him, tall as he was. He was almost a godly figure, walking the streets, the way people would stop or honk their horns at him, just react. He didn't back down from anybody. Nobody on the street. He didn't care. That's the way I figure it. Where he came from, you don't get no lower and harder than that. He'd get right in anybody's face. What he didn't understand, I guess, is that some of those people might be carrying pistols . . . but he didn't care. He'd go anywhere."

Manute would wear one of his two sweatsuits or maybe his one pair of pants with their 1970s bellbottoms. Always sneakers. On one of the explorations, Bradley remembers that both he and Manute bought so-called gold chains from a street peddler outside a place called Bogart's. The price was $10 apiece. The chains were greeted at the gym with great derision. Real gold? For $10? Bradley and Manute both denied that they had been conned by a rip-off artist. Bradley played basketball, sweated a bit, then his chain suddenly rusted. Manute played basketball, sweated, the chain stayed gold. Bradley has always wondered if Manute somehow did buy gold. Why didn't his chain rust?

"We're in a bar called Becky's one night," Bradley says. "We're having some beer. Manute, Deng, another African guy named Moquit, and myself. A guy starts making tall jokes about Manute. One tall joke after another. Manute gets mad, starts yelling at the guy. They go through the whole thing, a lot of F-Us. Manute finally leaves with Deng. Moquit and I stayed. Well, the guy pulls a knife on Moquit. Just like that. I know he wouldn't have pulled it on Manute. He would have been scared. But Moquit? Moquit just dropped to the floor and crawled out of the place, fast as he could before the guy got him. I was right after him."

English, basketball, hanging out, home to the In Town Apartments. That was Manute's routine. He spent a lot of time watching television. He said he was lonely sometimes, very lonely. He was cold. He said he was never scared. Why be scared? This was what he wanted to do. This was his choice. He did not have many clothes, mostly wearing warm-up suits. Later, someone provided a down jacket to fight the cold. Arlene Bialic bought him a sweater. He still did not have teeth.

"What about the teeth?" an academic counselor asked Mackey one day.

"Basketball first," Mackey said. "Then teeth."

"That's the thing about the NCAA," Mackey says. "If you're a parent and your kid has a toothache, what do you do? You send him to the dentist. What if the kid doesn't have a parent? What if he doesn't have teeth? Jerry Tarkanian said he gave his kid $200 a week spending money when the kid went to the University of Nevada at Las Vegas. He asked, 'What about the kids who don't have someone to give them $200 a week? What about them?'

"Ah, the NCAA . . . I was really hoping Jerry would win it when he played against Duke in the finals. Duke is fine, does everything right, but how many of those kids are out there?

Calvin Hill's son. How many middle-class kids are out there like him, kids who grow up with books in the house, with someone to turn off the television, with a quiet place to go to study? How many are great basketball players? Shouldn't there be something for all of these other kids who play? How many Dukes are there? These other kids need a place to play. There should be a Duke, but there also should be a Cleveland State."

The language classes continued into September and into the new season. Manute would not be eligible. He would not be an immediate Cleveland State student, a shock wave on the college basketball scene. The plan now was expanded to an entire year of English. Bialic was still doubtful. A year did not seem like enough. To take someone who had never been to any school, who had never written a word? To make him eligible for certified admission to college? She doubted it could ever be done, no matter how many years were involved.

Then, in February, in the middle of it all, Manute's father died of malaria. He had been dead for three weeks when Manute heard the news. He left immediately for the Sudan. His father had already been buried by the time he arrived. What to do? He grieved. His culture said that he was now responsible for the welfare of his sister, his mother's only other child. What to do? He decided that he could help her better—she was nineteen years old, a grown woman now, six feet eight herself—if he were a successful professional basketball player. He thought, more than ever, that this was a possibility. Hadn't he played already with professional basketball players, blocked their shots, sent their "weak shit into the cheap seats," as they might say? He would go back.

To his surprise, he suddenly had trouble leaving his country. The political atmosphere had changed. The Second Civil War had begun. In 1983 the fundamentalist Muslim law of *sharia* had been established. All the alcohol in the country had been dumped into the Nile River. The alligators became drunk. True. The punishment for drinking alcohol now was flogging. The punishment for petty theft was amputation. The administration of dictator Jaafar al Nimeiri was back at war with the Dinka and the other tribes of the south. Manute presented his passport and it was suddenly unacceptable. All of those little jokes about his age and his height—"Five feet two. I was sitting down."—now became sticky points. He explained that the national team had always taken care of his passport, that he had been in the army when he received it. The army had taken care of it. He had to wait six weeks for the technicalities to be resolved in the slow, bureaucratic way of the Middle East. He vowed to himself as he left that he would not return to the country until Nimeiri had been deposed, until the Dinka were part of the government of their own country.

Back at Cleveland, the pace of his education in the English language had been destroyed. He had gone backwards. There were doubts about whether he would be eligible to play the next season. There were doubts he would ever be eligible, so much to overcome. The school applied for a special waiver from the NCAA and was denied. Would he have to go through another year without formal competition, not starting on a basketball career that was now, with his sister to think about, even more important? He stayed in Cleveland through another summer, playing in the hot pickup games, studying English. He went to Boston, worked out at the Shelburne Recreation Center for Bill Musselman, coach of the Albany Patroons of the Continental Basketball Association. The signs were not good for the next season at Cleveland State. Manute decided to leave. He found out about the University of Bridgeport from Don Feeley. He and Deng left. The great secret was a secret no more.

"I was always hoping we could get him to play," Mackey says. "I don't think he was a secret. The people who lived in Cleveland knew all about him. He was here for a year. He came to our games. He was involved with the things around our team. How could he be a secret? He was part of the family.

"If he could have played . . . put it this way, if he could have come to this country when he was fifteen years old, with this country's nutritional standards, with coaching, with some inner-city competition . . . they would have had to change the rules for him. How good was he? Even as he was? The Cavs came to our gym. I saw him block NBA shots. All the time. I knew he could play in the NBA. He could have played in the NBA when he was here. All these guys who said he would never play, they didn't see him in that gym."

The run-and-stun juggernaut rolled anyway, even without Manute. The 1984–85 team finished at 21–8. The 1985–86 team—Manute now in the pros—brought Cleveland State into the sunshine with its postseason run. The upset of Indiana. The close loss to David Robinson. The king of Cleveland. The 1986–87 team added another, solid 25–8 season. The fallout from the Manute experiment—if experiment was the proper term—did not arrive until 1987. December 8, 1987, to be exact. The NCAA placed Cleveland State on probation for three years, banning the basketball team from the tournament for two seasons and from television for one.

This was the beginning of the nine-page report:

> In May 1983, Cleveland State University recruited and transported to the campus from a foreign country two prospective student-athletes, one of whom was of extraordinary height. During a stopover on the trip in Boston, Massachusetts, the men's basketball coach introduced the young men to an individual who became a representative of the institution's athletic interests when he provided local automobile transportation and entertained the young men and the head coach at his home and in his house during the stopover. Upon arrival at the campus for what the institution has contended was to be an official visit, but which the young men

reported as being for the purpose of enrollment, the young men were housed at a local hotel. Neither young man returned home. Rather, they both were housed, partially at university expense, in a hotel from May 23 to June 17, 1983, and both then moved into a housing facility that was used by the athletics department for student-athletes.

It was quickly determined when the young men arrived on campus that one of the prospective student-athletes lacked English language skills and also might not satisfy NCAA 2.000 academic certification requirements. The other prospective student-athlete had no such difficulties and was admitted to the university, awarded athletically related aid as a men's basketball team manager, and permitted to enroll for the summer term.

The university initiated correspondence with the NCAA seeking to establish eligibility for the primary prospect. Institution staff members transported him to an English-language program associated with a nearby university in order for the young man to enroll in the program, and institutional staff members routinely transported the prospect to the language classes. The men's head basketball coach subsequently had a conversation with the representative of the university's athletics interests who had met the prospect in Boston (who also was an agent for at least one professional basketball player) and informed the representative of financial difficulties the prospect was encountering. During this conversation, the representative stated that he would assist the young man. This representative has acknowledged that he helped pay substantial costs for language classes and living expenses for the prospect. Moreover, from July 1983 to June 1984, when requests for payment of fees by the English-language program administrators were received in the men's basketball office, members of the institutional staff, most frequently a men's assistant basketball coach, would deliver payments, usually in the form of money orders.

Although institutional staff members maintain that they had no intention of seeking admission for this prospect at

Cleveland State University and merely were trying to help the young man become proficient in English in order that they could help him gain admission to another institution, no evidence has been presented to indicate that such assistance was provided throughout the 15 months that the prospective student-athlete was in Cleveland. In fact, contrary to this position, on August 29, 1984, the athletics staff person charged with institutional compliance and certification regarding NCAA matters submitted a letter to the NCAA legislative services department informing that office that the prospective student athlete: (1) had become sufficiently proficient in English to score high enough on a GED test to be certified eligible under NCAA rules; (2) had by virtue of the GED test qualified for athletics eligibility at the school; and (3) was being awarded a scholarship at the university. . . .

The courtroom language turned a lark, a delicious scam, into a basketball felony. What was the big deal? A free meal in Boston? The meal was at Catapano's pizza place. Some money for room and board, for English lessons? Who was getting hurt? Certainly not the "student-athlete of extraordinary height." If anything, some good was being done here. Three years probation? Two years out of the tournament? The investigation had been proceeding since the spring of 1985, witnesses called, hearings held, so there had been an idea something was going to happen. No one had pictured something this serious.

Mackey had not helped matters. Never a fan of the NCAA, he had been less than forthcoming, evading all questions that could be evaded. It was the Somerville, kid-on-the-corner mentality: Don't give anything away to authority. He was not contrite. He argued. Why should the NCAA be bothering with Cleveland State, which was taking kids nobody wanted, giving them an education and a chance? Why go for the small potatoes? Why wasn't the NCAA investigating the real crooks, the big-time, headline monoliths who are in the tournament every year, signing all the big names out of the high schools, cheating all the way, yet never touched by scandal?

"Tell us who these people are," the investigators said.

"Find them yourselves," Mackey replied. "Just go to the parking lots. See what kids are driving what cars. Kids from the third floor of housing projects. You tell me how they got those cars."

"I said, 'What are you talking about?' " Mackey says. "The kid never played. A scholarship for a manager? Come on. I had a brother, played football at Harvard. He got the $100 handshake after every game. There was a guy, lived on the North Shore. My brother and a couple of other players went there every month. Had dinner, played with the guy's sons. The guy gave them money. The guy helped them find jobs. He was terrific. My father died, God bless him, and the guy was there at the wake, offering help. That's Harvard. If that's Harvard, what's everybody else? It goes right up the ladder."

The school appealed. The appeal was denied in April 1988 in an expanded forty-eight-page report that chronicled a number of "can't remember," "don't recall," and "I don't know" answers by Mackey and his assistant coaches and various members of the Cleveland State athletic department. The NCAA took exception to these responses, especially a "don't recall" by an assistant coach to a question about whether or not he had ever played in a pickup game against Manute, which would be an infraction.

"The committee considered the assistant coach's responses concerning this matter to be of utmost significance during its deliberations," the report read. "The committee does not accept that playing basketball with a 7'7" prospect who weighed 185 pounds and who did not speak English would be forgotten."

Cleveland State went on probation. Mackey went on a course that landed him in rehab, out of a job, embarrassed, humble.

*   *   *

The timing was unbelievable. The two years of ineligibility for the tournament passed. The sanctions were lifted. Mackey signed a new, two-year, $300,000 contract with the school on Wednesday, July 11, 1990. He said at a press conference, "I feel like I'm getting out of jail." On Thursday, he celebrated. The celebration continued into Friday. Friday night he was arrested outside a known Cleveland crack house and placed inside a real jail. The king's kingdom was no more.

"I was an alcoholic," he says now. "I didn't know it, but I was. It never interfered with my work, but I was always thinking about finishing up and having that drink. Medicating myself was the primary objective of the day. I was very clever. Alcoholics are very clever. I never stayed in one place too long. A couple of drinks, then I'd move along to somewhere else. I never had a DUI, because when I was drinking I drove very slow. I had seven speeding tickets, though. Those were when I was sober. I was on my way to drink."

The dual lives of an alcoholic fit into his nomadic search for basketball players very well. He could be the suburban husband, the father sending a son off to Harvard and two daughters to Boston College. He could also be the late-night rover. The recruiting trips took longer and longer to complete. A few rumors had begun to surface at the school about his drinking, but he charmed his way out of them. He had his suit-and-tie life. He had his ghetto life, arriving in the big ride, a celebrity.

"I started out on Thursday night going to a summer-league game," he says. "I had the six-pack in a cooler in the trunk of the car. I started going to some bars. It all gets hazy."

Somewhere in his travels he met two women. He was with them in the morning when he arrived at Cleveland State to pick up his first paycheck from the new contract. He was drunk. A television interview was taking place, concerning the case of a black professor who was suing the school for racial discrimination. The interviewer asked Mackey to comment about whether or not the case would affect recruiting. Mackey stared into the camera. The women waved and smiled behind him. He said he would not have a problem because "I develop a rapport with the mothers and aunts." He winked. The women were black.

The police were tipped later in the day that he was in the crack house. They waited outside. The television stations heard the news on the police scanner and sent crews. The crews waited. Half of them, the information on the police scanner hazy, thought they were waiting for Kevin Mack, a Cleveland Browns running back who had been involved in other drug problems. A friend, Alma Massey, arrived to convince Mackey to leave the place. She did not know about all the activity outside. Mackey finally relented and walked to his blue Lincoln town car with her. They drove no more than twenty feet before they were surrounded by police. The camera crews followed the police.

"Where's ESPN?" Mackey asked the cameras as he came out of the car.

Asked to take a Breathalyzer test, he squirted mouthwash into his throat, making any test useless. This meant he had to take a urinalysis. This test later showed the presence of cocaine in his body. Mackey was arrested on misdemeanor charges of driving under the influence and consuming alcohol in a motor vehicle. Massey, later called "a known prostitute" in the newspapers, was arrested when a syringe and spoon were reportedly found in her pocketbook. It was a mess. Six days later, Mackey was fired by Cleveland State. The press conference was shown live on Cleveland television. All other programming was preempted.

The charges from the arrest were handled with a sixty-day stay at an alcohol treatment center in Ohio, where he washed floors and scrubbed dishes and went through a mandatory recovery program. He went from Ohio directly into Lucas's program in Houston. Lucas called him and asked him to come.

"I'd never met him," Lucas, a former NBA guard and former drug user, says. "I just saw the story on television and decided to give him a call. I saw the pain on his face. It was a pain I know very well."

Manute, while with the Sudanese national basketball team.

Manute dunking during practice at the Catholic Club in Khartoum.

On the day Manute arrived in the United States: Manute, Kevin Mackey, Deng Nihal, and Don Feeley.

Manute with Bruce Webster at Bridgeport.

Publicity photo from Manute's year at Bridgeport.

Manute and Spud Webb, with the Rhode Island Gulls of the USBL.

Manute with Frank Catapano.

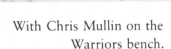

With Chris Mullin on the
Warriors bench.

Charles Barkley keeps Manute
out of a fight.

Dispensing food in Kenya, 1990.

Posing before the Capitol with a bowl of rice, the night of
Oxfam America's Hunger Banquet.

13

With his wife Atong and son Chris.

Bill Sheehan with
Manute's son Madut
and daughter Abouk.

14

His days now are a succession of small steps back toward basketball. He would like to move into the pro basketball structure somewhere, freed of all the rules and regulations and posturings of the college game. He apparently is going to be divorced. He is clean of alcohol, clean of all intoxicants. He says he feels, physically, better than he has at any time since he was sixteen years old. He is awake at six o'clock in the morning. He is talking at Alcoholics Anonymous meetings three times a week. He is without a basketball team to coach for the first time in his adult life, but he might be doing more important work here. Lucas is working with him on reshaping his personality, cutting out the good-time con, the short-cut approach to everything. This might be the biggest habit to kick of all.

"I want him to pay the right price," Lucas says. "If something costs $2.89, I don't want him trying to figure out how to get it for $2.88. The angles. I want him to forget the angles. Kevin had a problem with that when he came here. Like the phone. When he came here we didn't want him using the phone. We wanted him to be alone with his thoughts. So I'd point at the phone and say, 'Kevin, did you use the phone?' Kevin would say, 'No, I didn't use *that* phone.' Well, he didn't. But he was using other phones like crazy. Now, was he telling the truth? Yes. He didn't use *that* phone. But was he being totally honest? No. That's what we've been working on."

Mackey listens to the story. He is sitting in Lucas's office. The walls are filled with basketball pictures of famous players, all of them posed with Lucas's son except one. That one shows Lucas in a Milwaukee Bucks uniform. He is bent, hands on knees, along the foul lane. Standing next to him is Manute, a Washington Bullet. Manute is standing as tall as can be. The picture is above Mackey's head. Mackey smiles.

What can he say? He used the phones.

The giant next went to Bridgeport. Bridgeport? He performed his tricks with the round ball for the first time in public. Some people were amazed. Some people laughed. The giant did not mind. He had a plan. The man from the Great Outside said he would become rich and famous. This was a start.

Wasn't it? His picture was in the newspaper.

The school is dying. The athletic department is already dead. Bruce Webster is looking for a job. He has been the head basketball coach at the University of Bridgeport for twenty-seven seasons. His 1990–91 team finished second in the NCAA Division II tournament. Doesn't matter. This is a Thursday. Six days earlier, the trustees of the school announced that all athletic programs would cease at the end of this season. His present team's record is 21–6. The school is bankrupt. He is fifty-five years old. He is looking for a job.

"I'm applying for everything that's open," he says. "I've applied at Central Missouri, Winthrop College, Lewis University. I heard today there might be something at Southern Utah."

He never thought he was going to stay so long at the school. He had arrived as a young coaching whiz after three years as an assistant at Rutgers. His plan was to stick around for three or four years, then move along to a Division I job and big-time glory. That was the way careers went at the time: Big-time schools wanted coaches with small-time experience as a head coach. Somewhere in the middle, though, the rules changed. Big-time schools wanted big-time assistants simply to move to that final chair on the bench. Small-time experience was just that: small time.

Eventually he had stopped looking. Why move? He had a family, three kids. He had local success. His son went to Harvard. He liked where he worked, liked the area. He could go out the front door of Harvey Hubbell Gymnasium and look across Seaside Park and see Long Island Sound. Why move? Only in the last few years was there desperation. As the school floundered, sacrifices were made. His salary was cut from a high of $44,000 to a low of $29,000. His medical benefits were cut in half. The school's contribution to his pension plan was cut from 10 percent to 3 percent. He had always sold real estate to augment his income. Now he also started driving a Connecticut Limousine bus back and forth from LaGuardia Airport in New York on weekends.

"The school didn't plan right," he says. "We're down from eight thousand to three thousand students and we have fifty buildings on campus. Fifty buildings. That many students, you need maybe four. Everything changed. The education bubble burst. They were planning here for a great expansion that never came. They have a huge library here, a gift. Fine. They never realized that it would cost $150,000 a year just to heat and maintain the thing. They don't have that kind of money now."

The interviews by the Connecticut media all week have been sad ones, obituaries while the season continues. He is sick of the obituaries. He would rather talk about Manute. Manute was a much happier time. An assistant dean, a fan, is in the office. He is wondering how much of the story can be told because some illegalities might be involved. Webster says all of the story can be told. He laughs.

"What are they going to do?" he asks. "Put us on probation?"

"Donald Feeley is my best friend in the world," Webster says. "He coached at Sacred Heart in Bridgeport when I began coaching here. We've always been friends. I knew about Manute in Cleveland, about all of the stuff, about how Donald wound up without a job. I knew Manute was taking the classes at Case Western in English Language Studies. I knew Kevin Mackey was trying to convince him to stay for a second year at Case, because he still didn't know English well enough to attend Cleveland State. Manute calls Donald and says he wants out, that he wants to go to a school where he can play. Donald calls me. As it turns out, we also have an ELS program."

Webster went to the admissions director, a friend. He asked the friend—hypothetically, of course—if it would be possible to enroll a basketball player, an African male, the tallest man in the world, in the ELS program at Bridgeport even if the man could not read or write. The admissions director asked Webster what he had been smoking. Webster asked his question again. The admissions director said it might be possible. The tallest man in the world. The admissions director thought it all was a joke.

The process of getting Manute and, of course, Deng from Cleveland became strung out and secretive. It was being done without Mackey's knowledge. Webster made his calls to Cleveland only under a pseudonym. Letters were written. One month passed. Another. Finally, two plane tickets were sent. Webster and Feeley went to meet the plane at LaGuardia.

"We're forty-minutes late," Webster says. "I'm in a panic. We come into the terminal and there must be twenty different gates, maybe three thousand people. I think we'll never find Manute. It's terrible. Feeley takes one look over the heads of the crowd and says, 'He's not here.' I say, 'What do you mean, he's not here?' Feeley says, 'Not here.' We go downstairs to baggage claim and here is my first view of Manute. I'd never seen him. He is leaning against a wall, wearing this enormous raincoat. A little old woman, must have been eighty-five, is pulling at the hem of the raincoat. She is saying, 'How tall are you? You're a very tall person, do you know that? How tall? Are you on stilts?' Manute is saying, 'Get away from me. Go.' That is my first view."

One strange view led to another. Webster noticed that the entire airport stopped when Manute walked toward the door. Baggage handlers. Passengers. Workers. Stopped. Webster noticed a cabdriver outside was staring so hard that he ran over a curb and into a post. It was something out of a cartoon. Webster noticed that Manute, sitting in the front seat of the car, was so squashed his knees literally touched the roof. Every half hour on the ride home, Webster would have to stop the car on the side of the Connecticut Turnpike. Manute would unfold, jog around the car a half-dozen times to restore circulation, then pack himself back into the seat.

For the first five days at Bridgeport, Manute stayed at Webster's house, hidden, sleeping on two beds pulled together lengthwise in the basement. The neighborhood kids staked out the front porch, hoping for a sight of him. When he appeared, he posed for pictures with everyone. Webster introduced Manute to the admissions director, who acted as if he had seen a daydream suddenly come to life, but said he would get to work. Manute himself had only one request. He said he liked to play basketball every day.

"So I take him over to the gym," Webster says. "I'm trying hard to keep inside the NCAA rules, so I know I can't stay and watch him practice. I bring out a ball and throw it to him. I tell him I am going to my office. As I turn around—as I turn around!—I see him take the ball, reach up, and almost without leaving his feet, dunk the ball in the basket. Just like that. I say, 'Forget it, we'll never lose a game.' I go to my office with a big smile and start calling everyone I know. Friends. Relatives. I'm just calling. I come out about forty-five minutes later. I left Manute alone. Now there must be five hundred people in here watching him. Everyone from the park across the street, everyone from the neighborhood. Word got out that fast."

The admissions director did his job. He told the admissions board that the meeting was not being held to decide whether or not Manute Bol should be admitted to the University of Bridgeport. It was being held to decide *how* Manute Bol would be admitted to the University of Bridgeport. The minimum requirement on a test for admission to the ELS program was supposed to be 17 or 19 and Manute had a 12 or 13, something like that, but, well . . . that was fine. The visa question was obvious, but, well, there was something called a JV13 where an applicant would promise to return to his native land for at least two years of service.

"Would Manute be willing to do that?" Webster was asked.

"Oh, sure, no problem," Webster said.

Webster fashioned Manute's college schedule personally. He explained Manute's particular problems—poor English and an inability to read or write—to each instructor. Would the instructor be willing to help a student with these somewhat unique university problems? A geology professor said he would give Manute oral exams if Manute promised to attend every minute of every class. A pottery professor said clay was a universal language of the hands. Photography was another course. Gem-cutting was a fourth. For a fifth course, Manute took raquetball. Webster was the instructor.

"What Manute had was an entire schedule of electives," Webster says. "I will say this for him. He never missed a minute of any class. He never missed a minute of his ELS classes every morning either. Do you know what he wound up with? A 2.8 out of 4.0."

Somewhere during the enrollment process, but before the official announcement of Manute's arrival, word seeped back to Cleveland about where he had landed. Mackey contacted Catapano. Catapano contacted Feeley. Feeley contacted Webster. The entire business suddenly took on a sinister look. Feeley called at eleven o'clock at night. Catapano and a Cleveland State assistant named Leo Papile had tracked Feeley down at the Milford Jai Alai fronton. They were with him now as he asked Webster to come to the Stratford Motor Inn for a meeting. It all seemed strange. Webster's instincts told him not to go. His wife told him not to go. Of course, he went.

"You can leave now, Don," Catapano told Feeley when Webster reached the room. "We want to talk to Bruce alone."

"I'll see you later," Feeley said.

"What do you mean, you'll see me later?" Webster said. "You go home and I'll call you in an hour. If I don't call, send the police up here immediately."

Webster did not know either of the men. His immediate thought was that they belonged to the Mafia. They were both Italian, both big. He says Catapano did nothing to change the impression, coming in with a hard, angry approach. Papile sat in the background. Webster says Catapano said he already had over $10,000 invested in Manute and now Manute had been stolen. He wanted Manute back. If this did not happen, there could be some serious consequences. He knew people who knew people. Webster says he replied that it was too late, that all of the papers had been signed and Manute was now enrolled at Bridgeport. It would be illegal to have him return to Cleveland. He would also be ineligible.

"It was a bad scene for a while," Webster says. "I didn't know this guy. After a while, though, it became respectable and three days later, when I drove my son to Harvard, I had lunch with

Frank. You know what? We started talking. I'm from Mineola, Long Island. He's from Mineola. I went to Mineola High School. He went to Chaminade, across the street. I started naming some names and I knocked his socks off. It turned out . . . he wasn't with any mob. He was just talking. We actually became friends. He wound up representing some kids I've had here at the school."

A final call came from Mackey. Webster had known Mackey from New England basketball. Mackey had virtually recruited Bagley from the Bridgeport gym. Mackey said that things happen and no one was hurt. He wished Manute good luck at Bridgeport.

The arrival of Manute on the small school's campus brought instant notoriety. A press conference was held in the gymnasium to introduce him to the media. Ten folding chairs were put on the floor, circling a table. More than a hundred media people appeared. Webster had thought about keeping Manute off limits, unavailable for interviews, but ran a test with a sportscaster friend, Rob Michaud. Michaud came back and said Manute was a wonderful interview. No problem. Manute told his stories of having his teeth removed and about how he had the scars cut into his head, and about the time he killed a sleeping lion with a spear one afternoon in the bush. ("Of course, he was sleeping. I would not fight a lion who is awake.")

"The response was amazing," Webster says. "We had five dentists on the phone the next day, offering to provide Manute with bridgework for free. People were offering everything. They wanted Manute to appear at stores, to sign autographs, pose for pictures. There were all kinds of opportunities. Manute couldn't take any of them."

The NCAA would allow no special help. To get Manute's teeth fixed, Webster enrolled him in a welfare dental plan. For fifteen consecutive Mondays, Webster and Manute and Deng sat in the welfare clinic, getting the work done. A man appeared with a custom-made wooden bed, eight feet long, painted in the school color, purple. Manute's name was written in white on the head-board. Unacceptable. A gift. To get Manute a bed, the school had to purchase six extra-long beds and make them available to all students. Manute was given one. No one knows who wanted the other five. Crazy.

"Eventually, the bed the guy made, the purple one, was put up for a phone-in auction on public television," Webster says. "I wanted Manute to have it as a memory of his time here. He was now in Washington. I watched the show and started bidding."

The bidding went crazy. Webster found himself matched against another caller and dropped out when the price reached $500. The other bidder turned out to be Michaud, the sports announcer, who also wanted Manute to have the bed. If the two men hadn't been bidding against each other, the price would have been $50. They split the cost and sent the bed to Manute.

"There were so many little things," Webster says. "He didn't like the cafeteria food and we tried to have some different meals for him and that didn't work either. I took him down to Artie's Famous Pizza. I introduced him to Artie, who's a friend and has always liked Bridgeport basketball. I asked Artie if he could feed Manute every night, just let him come in and eat. Artie looks at him and says, 'You look like a good kid to me, Manute. I'll do it. As long as you're a good kid, Manute, you just come here and eat.' Manute went there every night. That was his training table. Pizza and beer. He loved the beer."

Manute had one faded leisure suit. That was his wardrobe. Another Webster friend, a salesman for Puma sneakers, provided six warm-up suits. That was all Manute wore, every day. The warm-up suits and sneakers. He had no shoes. A girl in one of his classes was the daughter of a Jordache jeans executive. She eventually provided two special pairs of Jordache jeans. Every need was slowly met. Webster was worried about Manute's lack of weight, so he took him to the doctor for a physical. The doctor found hookworms were living in Manute's body. The hookworms were treated. Everyone expected an instant weight gain. None arrived. The doctor said that if Manute was young, he should be gaining weight, but if he was, say, twenty-four or twenty-five, his weight probably had stabilized. How old was he?

"We do need a diploma and a birth certificate," Webster told Deng.

"No problem," Deng said. "Two days."

The diploma and birth certificate arrived. They were written in Arabic on normal-looking paper. Webster tried to figure out the words on the diploma.

"Is this a real school?" he asked Deng.

"Sure," Deng said. "Unfortunately, it burned down a couple of years ago."

The season was different from any season any small-college team had ever played. The small gymnasiums of New England were packed whenever Bridgeport visited. A motorcycle escort would take the team in and out of the cities. The home games were also packed, every game sold out at Harvey Hubbell (capacity 1,800). Webster found himself working eighteen-hour days. There was no public relations apparatus at the school. All the interviews, all the requests, went through him. He was tied to this out-of-control tornado. He loved it.

"Our first game is at home," he says. "Stonehill. Manute scores 20 points, has twenty rebounds, blocks six shots. Crazy. No one had ever seen anyone like him. All kinds of media. Crazy. Our next game is on the road, at Springfield. Now, there are two kinds of buses you can get when you rent. One is the forty-seven-seater, the other is the forty-nine-seater. The forty-nine-seater has the long seat in the back, all the way across, so Manute could sit in the middle and stretch his legs down the aisle. Well, the first game, we get a forty-seven-seater. There's nowhere he can fit.

The bus is packed, too, because everyone wants to go to the game. I throw my car keys to my assistant coach and tell him to take Manute in my car and follow the bus. I keep turning around, watching, and suddenly I see my car pull over to the side. I forgot. He has to get out and jog around the car to get his circulation going.

"We get the police escort and everything, the press is waiting in Springfield . . . and no Manute. Finally, he shows up at the gym. We get the forty-nine-seater for every game after that."

The idea on the floor was simply to give Manute the ball and let him dunk or be fouled. The normal Division II center is a foot shorter than Manute. Teams practiced for Manute by having their center hold a broom to simulate his arms reaching high in the air. Manute was usually a tall, thin man on a floor filled with small, nasty children. Webster researched the way Division I teams had used famous, enormous people, especially the way the University of Virginia had used Ralph Sampson. He invented his own tricks for this situation.

Manute had trouble handling a bounce pass, looking down. So there were no bounce passes. Simple enough. The smaller college foul lane was perfect. Manute could set himself for rebounds simply with one step underneath. He would be where he wanted to be. There were various strategies for getting the ball to him, but the most obvious one was simply to shoot. What the heck. Maybe the ball would go in. Manute would be there for the rebound if it didn't. Teams tried every defense known to basketball against him, boxes and ones, triangles and two, players sagging all over him, playing in front of him, in back of him, playing at every angle possible.

The one problem was the lack of a shot clock in Division II at the time. Teams finally decided the best way to play against him was not to play, to hold the ball for as long as possible. By the second half of the season, every team was holding the ball against Bridgeport.

"Our first games in the season, we averaged in the 80s and

90s," Webster says. "Our last games, we were down to the 30s and 40s. Everybody was holding. If there had been a shot clock, he would have been unstoppable. We would have won every game, easy. Holding the ball gave teams a chance."

Every game was a special small-college event that probably would not happen again. Strangely, there was not the malice toward the big visitor there would normally be for an out-sized opponent in road gyms. A sense of wonder surrounded him, a sense of good fun. Who could be mad at someone so tall and so thin and from so far away? A fraternity from Quinnipiac, a rival, even proposed a party for Manute. The fraternity wanted to make him its Man of the Year. Webster received the letter.

"What do you think?" he asked Manute.

"I want to go," Manute replied. "Is it possible?"

"I have two conditions," Webster said. "First, we have to win the game. Second, if you go, everybody on the team has to go. If the fraternity invites everyone—and we win—we go."

In the Quinnipiac gym, a special section was roped off with a sign that read "Manute Bol Party Fans" on the night of the game. The gym held a thousand people; this section held two hundred. They were all Quinnipiac students, but they were all cheering for Manute. The Quinnipiac coach, Burt Kahn, was angry all night. Manute scored 22 points and blocked fifteen shots. Bridgeport rolled. The party was held in a large hall. The forty-nine-seat Bridgeport bus arrived. Everyone went. It was a perfect small-college moment.

"We're playing another game, at Mt. St. Mary's in Baltimore," Webster says. "We're in warm-ups. The coach, Jimmy Phelan, a friend of mine, says, 'You know, I had a seven-foot-five guy here once.' I say, 'No kidding.' He says, 'Do you know that guy with the metal teeth, who was the villain in the James Bond movies? That was my guy. Seven-five.' I say, 'Could he play?' Jimmy says, 'Nothing.' "

Their final record was 26–5. Manute averaged 22.5 points, 13.5 rebounds, and seven blocked shots. The final game came in the Division II Regionals. Bridgeport lost, 42–40, to a Sacred Heart team it had beaten three times during the regular season. It was another stall game, Sacred Heart inching into the lead and holding the ball to let the clock run. Webster was upset at the lack of foul calls, especially when Manute would set up for the special Bridgeport in-bounds play. The passer would simply throw the ball high into the air toward the basket. Manute would catch it and dunk. The shorter Sacred Heart players whacked at him and pushed him so he would not be free to catch the ball. The referees called nothing. They only called fouls once the clock was moving.

"Manute had the ball with six seconds left, we're trailing by two," Webster says. "He was fourteen feet from the basket. I was hoping he'd take the hook, but a kid broke to the basket and Manute spotted him and made the pass. The kid dropped the ball out of bounds. I still say no one would have come close if we'd had the shot clock in Division II. We'd have been national champions, unbeaten, easy."

The other players on the Bridgeport team went through the season as if it were a full-length fantasy cartoon. The ones who had played at the school a year earlier remembered crowds of two hundred people, when Webster's instructions were easy to hear, simply spoken from the bench. Now? From the first cryptic message in Webster's annual summer letter to encourage conditioning—"When you come back, there will be a big surprise waiting for you"—until the final disappointing game, the season was one continuous hoot.

"Here's the first time I saw Manute," forward Mark Farisi says. "First day of practice. I open the door to the gym. He's standing in front of me. I'm looking straight into his chest. And I'm six feet eight."

Who'd have thought this kind of player would ever play at

Bridgeport? John O'Reilly, one of the captains, had been leery when he'd heard the rumors. How could this be? Bridgeport? The guy had to be a stiff. Then he saw Manute. Then the practices began. How could this be? O'Reilly was soon throwing high lobs into the key and watching the ball being deposited in the basket.

"Manute was in one of my classes," O'Reilly says. "I'd sit next to him. His legs would be just spread out across three or four chairs."

In the beginning Manute seemed shy. He didn't have the teeth. He was making new friends. He mostly would appear with Deng at his side, Deng as a friend and translator. Deng had to sit out the season, because he was a transfer from Cleveland State, but he was still a full-time scholarship student. As days passed, as the teeth were delivered, as friends were made, Manute became more and more his own person. He roomed with Deng but went out with other groups, too. This was college. College life. He lived it well.

"What's college, anyway?" Farisi says. "Isn't it a time to go out, have a few beers, meet some interesting women? Isn't that what you did? Isn't that what everybody did? Manute and I got along really well, probably as well as anyone. We spent a lot of time together. I was a little older, because I'd gone a couple of years to Central Connecticut, dropped out, worked, and now I was starting school again. He was older. Our personalities just meshed.

"We'd go out every night. We kept count. I think the record was we once went out thirty-five straight nights, drinking beer. It was amazing to go with him. I didn't have any money. He didn't have any money. Somehow we'd go out every night and drink as much beer as we wanted, never pay a thing. How did that happen? I never figured it out. I met my wife with him. She stood on a chair in some bar to talk to us because we were so tall. That's the first time I met her."

Reservations gone, Manute would say he could do anything. Whatever game came on the television, Manute would say he could play it. Football? *I could do that.* Boxing? *I could be the heavyweight champion of the world.* Baseball? *Easy. I could do that.* His level of confidence, which had started him on this trip so far away, was now public. He felt he could be a success at anything he tried.

There would be grand tavern pool games. Pool? *I am the best pool player in history.* Minnesota Fats? Minnesota Manute. Video games? *Does anyone have a quarter?* There would be those late-night college conversations about home and friends and family. Farisi would talk about Lynn, Massachusetts. Manute would talk about the Sudan, about the death of his father, the plight of his sister, about smoking Marlboro cigarettes as a kid. Very proud. Sudan had Marlboro cigarettes. Topics could include politics and religion and that very nice-looking coed at the next table.

"Deng was interesting," Farisi says. "He knew English really well and had really adapted, but I think he'd watched too many Clint Eastwood movies. He'd say things to women like, 'Hey, baby, come on over here,' and 'Hey, sweetheart, why don't you join us?' You know those lines that guys use in the movies but no one says in real life? He really said them. I'd say, 'Deng, that isn't how it really works.' He'd keep using the same lines. Manute, though, he was cool. He just talked to women normal."

The games, the practices, were part of the ramble. Manute would keep score during the scrimmages. Someone would say the score was, say, 6–5. Manute would say, no, the score was 7–5. There would be an argument. The score would be 7–5. Manute would shout out names and encouragements. Manute would dunk. On the road, the story almost always would be the same. The first reaction of fans would be "whoaaaaaaa." The players could hear the people talking, see them pointing. The second reaction would be to cheer against Bridgeport and the big man. The third reaction, kicking in somewhere during the second half, would be to cheer for Bridgeport and the big man. It seldom varied.

"Manute would win everyone over," O'Reilly says. "How could you not root for him? You could see he was trying so hard."

"We'd be going home from the games, Manute in that last seat on the bus," Farisi says. "It'd be dark. All of a sudden, you'd hear Manute say in that low voice, 'Beer. Coach, beer.' *Screeech.* The bus would pull right over to the side. Pit stop! Beer! Coach Webster never allowed that before Manute and certainly didn't allow it after, but that season . . . the big man spoke. We stopped for beer."

On a winter night, during Christmas break, the team back at school early for games and practice, there was a classic snowball fight. Manute had been complaining of a sore knee during practice, had skipped most of the hard drills. Everyone was walking across campus. The fight began. Everyone started throwing snowballs at the easiest, biggest target. Manute became mad. He started a counterattack, snowballs in both hands.

"He's chasing us," O'Reilly says. "We're saying, 'Manute, what about your knee? Aren't you worried about your knee?' He looks like he's doing the hundred-meter dash in the Olympics. That knee isn't hurting him at all."

On most teams lines were usually drawn between white and black, cliques forming, steps taken in opposite directions, but there were no lines here. Guys were guys. Quiet might stick with quiet, funny with funny, but black and white were not part of the equation. Manute, in Farisi's words, was "just another knucklehead, a true knucklehead." The outside observers always seemed to describe his long journey, his otherworldly look, his troubles with the language and all the rest. His new teammates talked about his intelligence and wit, a lot about his wit. They took him to their homes for vacations. ("He comes in the door," Farisi says. "I had this old Siamese cat. The cat sees Manute, she must have jumped a hundred feet, straight up in the air.") Manute's conversations took his teammates to parts of the world they never imagined existed. It was an even swap. No one felt sad for anyone.

"We're playing, late in the season," Farisi says. "I never played too much. We're pounding someone in the second half and I go in and figure I'm going to take some shots. Every time I get the ball, I shoot. Coach calls time out. He says, 'Farisi, we got the biggest guy on the planet. Give him the ball, will you?' It was just so much fun. It was college the way it should be."

The planning for Manute's second season had already begun. Bridgeport was going to move into the big time. A three-game trip to Hawaii was scheduled. A game at UNLV. A game at Cal-Berkeley. A game at the Meadowlands. Negotiations were taking place to play some home games at Madison Square Garden. Webster found himself in conversations about situations he did not know existed.

"I'm talking with this assistant at Iowa," he says. "That's another place we're going to play. Iowa. I say that we'll probably be a good draw because of Manute—the guy says all home games are sold out for the season anyway. I promise that we won't hold the ball, that we'll come out and play—the guy says he isn't worried because Iowa will use its own refs. I start to talk about money, about how much money we'll get. I suggest $5,000 or maybe $8,000. The guy says he'll give us $14,000, guaranteed."

The planning then stopped. Just like that. Manute announced he was leaving school to turn pro, making himself eligible for the NBA draft.

Catapano urged him to stay for one more season. Webster urged. The pros were not exactly falling all over themselves coming after him. Only a couple of lower-level scouts had even bothered to see what all the noise was about at Bridgeport.

Manute simply said it was time to see if he could make some money. Who could argue with that? He wanted to send some money home to his sister, now that his father was dead. He had been in America for two years. He was not afraid of the pros. His English was fine.

"An administrator at the school, a woman, had become fond of Manute," Webster says. "She made a last pitch. She called him to her office and said the school would give him whatever he wanted. She said if he didn't want to go to classes, he wouldn't have to go. If he wanted his own room, he could have that. Whatever he wanted. He simply wanted to go. I called him in to give my blessing. I told him he could go, but he had to do one thing. He had to return the teeth to the school. He looked at me in shock. I said, 'It's a joke, Manute.' "

The school went back to its normal schedule, playing at Lowell in Massachusetts and Franklin Pierce in New Hampshire instead of Hawaii. The team became a normal team again, populated with kids who were a step slow or a few inches too short to play in the big time. There was sudden interest in the school from African players, but it didn't bring another Manute. Deng hurt a knee, had surgery, and was never the same player again, but he graduated. Another African, David Shokai, played. Webster said he turned down "at least twenty-five players" from Africa. He did take a flier a few years later on a kid from Nigeria. The flier made him forget Africa.

"It was a big scam," Webster says. "We get this clipping from a Nigerian paper. There's a picture of a guy blocking Hakeem Olajuwon's shot during some game in Lagos. The caption has the guy's name. There's another picture, a team picture of the Nigerian national team. The tallest guy is circled. His name in the caption is the same as the guy in the first picture. He's supposed to be six feet ten. We go through the entire procedure, getting him a visa, bringing him over here. He gets off the plane and he's six feet five, tops, and he can't dribble and chew gum at the same time. And he's not the guy in the picture. He comes to the school for about two weeks, then disappears into New York where he goes to live with a cousin illegally. It's all just a way to get into the country.

"Two months later another coach shows me the same pictures—the guy blocking Hakeem's shot, the team picture—only the captions are different. There is another name instead of the first guy's. Now the guy's name is Bananahead or something. Some group in Nigeria was falsifying all this stuff, trying to get kids into America. It was all a big con."

The NCAA's investigators also arrived after Manute left. There was a hearing in Duluth, Minnesota. Bridgeport was placed on probation for a year for its dealings with Manute. Webster had arguments for all of the moves that had been made. The NCAA picked the arguments apart with tweezers.

"It was all such little stuff," Webster says, still mad. "The big thing they had was that we went to New York to pick him up at the airport. That is against the rules. Well, how was he going to get to Bridgeport? The second thing—we said we had paid for the tickets because this was the one recruiting trip allowed—was that Manute had never returned home from the recruiting trip. Well, school was starting in four days. Where was he going to go? Back to the Sudan? Back to Cleveland? It was so silly that Deng, to stay eligible, had to pay back my wife $12.50 for a Christmas dinner she had cooked for him and Manute. He had to pay me $7.50 for a pair of galoshes that I had bought him as a Christmas present, because there was snow on the ground and all he and Manute had were sneakers. Just silly."

The money was repaid. The probation was served. Manute was gone.

"I worried about Manute when he left," Webster says. "I still worry about him. Is he saving any money? The one thing I said to Frank Catapano when Manute left was that I hoped he'd take whatever money he made and get maybe a $25,000 CD with good interest, have some money in the bank. I said I didn't want to see Manute in a year or two in a career as the world's tallest bellhop at the New York Hilton. Three years later, Manute signs the contract for $5.4 million. Frank calls me and says Manute still doesn't have the CD. He says Manute has the contract, but probably has about ten bucks in his pocket. Manute just likes to spend. I worry about him in the end."

Webster says there are bigger worries than Manute's finances, though, at the moment. Are there not? The school is dying. Dead.

"It's all over here," he says. "It's obituaries. I have to get these kids ready for the tournament. We're trying to pull off the Cinderella story of all time, win the national championship in the last game the school ever plays. Wouldn't that be something? This group of kids—the seniors—have done everything but that. It would be the great finale."

Across the wall of his office are black-and-white photographs of his twenty-seven teams. Manute's team is at the end of a row, Manute standing so much taller than everyone else. Various Coach of the Year citations are on other walls. Trophies are on bookcases. Twelve basketballs in a rack, the practice balls, are in a corner. Webster sits at his desk. His phone rings every now and then, colleagues offering condolences.

"Here's something," he says. "A couple of days ago, I became the winningest basketball coach in New England history."

Now he needs a job.

*The giant next went to Newport, Rhode Island.
This was a test. How good were his tricks with the
round ball? If the giant's tricks were not good
enough, he might have to leave the Great Outside.
Everyone else seemed to worry, but the giant did
not worry. He did his tricks. They were good, good
enough. He was on the way.*

He would be . . .

A star?

Kevin Stacom is a real-life Sam Malone, the character played
by Ted Danson on the television series "Cheers." The sport is
different—Malone supposedly pitched for the Red Sox, Stacom
played guard for the Celtics. The towns are different—Malone
supposedly manages the Cheers bar across from the Boston Common, Stacom manages The Mudville Cafe in Newport, Rhode
Island. The rest is the same. Stacom is the personable ex-jock,
forty years old, his black hair turned a totally premature gray,
greeting the familiar patrons and running the bar. He also works
in sales for a graphics design company during the day. He was an
English major at Holy Cross and Providence College, one of the
few English majors ever to play in the NBA. His last game was
in 1982.

In the spring of 1985, he was part owner of another bar, the Dockside, located in the heart of Newport's traffic, serving the tourists who arrived to visit the famous summer homes of the Astors and the Vanderbilts or to enjoy the beach and the sun. Newport is sort of a yuppie theme park, filled with shops that sell overpriced beach dresses and with restaurants and nightclubs that have boating motifs to attract sailors home from an afternoon on their luxury sailboats and yachts. It was once the permanent home to the America's Cup races before the Australians came along and won the damn thing and moved the action elsewhere. No matter. The America's Cup docks and boatyards have quietly been replaced by luxury time-share condominiums.

Stacom had spent the winter of 1984 as a second assistant coach at Northeastern University in Boston, probably his last blast at basketball, and was now back in Newport to tend to bar business. A proposition arrived.

"I was offered a chance to coach a Rhode Island team in this new spring basketball league, the USBL," he says. "I didn't know if I wanted to do it, but it sounded interesting. I talked with the owners a couple of times and then I went with them to a press conference at the Biltmore Hotel in Providence to announce the team. I was still thinking it over, whether or not I'd take the job, when the commissioner of the league gets up and says, 'And now I'd like to introduce the coach of the Rhode Island Gulls, Kevin Stacom.' I said, well, I guess I'd better get to work."

The Rhode Island Gulls. A different name, to be sure. A uniform shirt with a large cartoon seagull across the front, dropping a basketball from the sky. The first thought had been to play the games in Providence at the Civic Center, but at twelve thousand seats the building seemed too large and expensive. Newport seemed a perfect second choice. It was the location of the largest high school gym in the state—Rogers High School—and was a warm-weather attraction. Perhaps some of the yuppies could be persuaded to watch a little hoops after a long day wrestling with their jibs and spinnakers.

Stacom was the coach, general manager, and just about everything else for the Gulls. He set up the deal with the high school, called the printers about the posters, started to put together a roster. He wanted to build a team that promised fun, that was interesting to a jaded public. This was minor-league basketball, but he did not want it to look, in his words, "like Palookaville." He wanted a different sort of package.

"One of the players I was recruiting was a guard named Stu Primus," Stacom says. "He was from Boston College and I liked his body. I thought he had an NBA body. I thought this league might be good for him, because he wasn't rated too highly by the scouts. I made an appointment to see his agent, Frank Catapano, in Boston."

The meeting was at Catapano's pizza place. Stacom introduced himself. The discussion was all about Primus and the league and Stacom's thoughts about basketball. Stacom described how he was a believer in the running game, fast-break basketball, which he had played at Providence and with the Celtics. He said that some coaches were afraid of the fast break, with all of its turnovers and sometimes helter-skelter action, but that he thought in the long run fast-break basketball was winning basketball. A coach simply had to be prepared to squirm at some ugly-looking moments for a while, to forget the turnover stats and concentrate on the long haul. He repeated his hope for the Gulls, that they be different and interesting. Stacom was from New York and Catapano was from New York and they talked about New York. They talked about Boston. The meeting appeared to be finished. Primus was signed. Stacom stood to leave.

"Kevin," Catapano said. "Sit down. Listen, I also represent Manute Bol. I like what you say. I want him to play for you."

Stacom had never thought about Manute. The USBL had held a draft and the New Haven entry had picked Manute. Stacom was intrigued with Manute, to be sure. Who wouldn't be? He had seen films of Manute on television and liked his size (of course) and his agility for such a tall man, and his basketball sense. Stacom was already a semi-believer in Manute and definitely had an open mind. He also did not see how Manute could play for the Gulls. Manute belonged to New Haven.

"Kevin," Catapano said, "if he doesn't play for you, he doesn't play. That's it. He'll play for you. Believe me."

"What Frank had been doing all along, while we were talking about Primus, was feeling me out," Stacom says. "It was an audition. He wanted to see if I'd be all right to coach Manute. What he was afraid of was that Manute would wind up with some crazy coach whose only idea was to win every game and to win the league title. He wanted a guy who would play Manute for most of the game, showcase him. There were only about eight games before the NBA draft and this was going to be important for Manute. He had to show what he could do. Not many people were interested in him at that point. He'd played in a New England all-star game against Division I players and hadn't looked too good. A lot of people had written him off as a curiosity who couldn't play. Frank wanted to make sure Manute would be seen. I said that I didn't have any problem with that. Didn't I want an interesting team?"

Catapano had lobbied for a second season at Bridgeport, but once Manute made up his mind, the agent was going to try to find the best opportunity available. There was a certain pressure. Suppose Manute wasn't taken in the NBA draft? Suppose he didn't make the NBA? What did he do then? Presumably he could play in the Continental Basketball League, with a minor league season that ran parallel to the NBA's. Or maybe Europe. Or somewhere. The idea, though, always had been the NBA. The Bridgeport successes didn't seem to count. Nobody had paid attention. Something had to be done to win NBA hearts and minds. Something had to be done in a hurry. The USBL season would begin on May 25 and run into the middle of August, but the NBA draft was in June. Eight games. That was showtime. The rest could be for practice, for learning.

Manute was introduced as a Gull at a press conference at

Stacom's bar. The bar was packed. Stacom had not seen Manute in person until that moment. He was astounded. He was good friends with Hank Finkel, who was seven feet tall and played with the Celtics. He had never noticed Finkel's height twice. Manute? Stacom stared. Everyone stared. Stacom found it to be an embarrassing moment.

"I took Manute to the back room for a few minutes, just to get everyone calmed down," he says. "It wasn't that people were being ignorant. They just hadn't seen anyone like Manute. They couldn't control themselves."

In filling out his interesting field, Stacom took some other chances. He contacted the agent for five-foot-seven Spud Webb. At the opposite end of the height charts, Webb was also not regarded as an NBA prospect. He had played point guard at North Carolina State in a successful program that used a slow-down, patterned offense. Stacom thought Webb was miscast and would be much better in a pro, running game. He was surprised to learn that Webb was already on a barnstorming tour throughout North Carolina, packing small high school gyms because his jumping and scoring feats were legendary. The agent said the Gulls would be a fine opportunity for Webb. Another pick was six-foot-ten John (Hot Rod) Williams, a certified potential NBA talent, but under indictment for allegedly fixing games in college at Tulane. No one wanted to be associated with Williams. Stacom did.

"I read a story about him," Stacom says. "It was a sad thing. I remember the picture of him, sitting next to a barn or something at his father's farm back home. I read about the charges. I'd been around enough in this game, was cynical enough, that I thought I could see what was really happening. I wanted to give the kid a chance. I called his lawyer, who was a good guy. The lawyer told me more about the case, about how the two kids testifying against him had been betting and involved with drugs and how they were now being given immunity. He talked about a district attorney who was trying for a reputation by going after the biggest name. It sounded right to me. I said that we weren't paying a lot of money, but this would be a good place for the kid to get away from his troubles, to get in a good workout and play against some good people. The lawyer agreed with me. He said John would be there."

The English kid, Martin Clark, a Kevin Mackey recruit who'd made headlines by scuffling on the sidelines with head coach Gary Williams at Boston College, was signed. A local guy named Owen Wells, who'd played a bit for the Houston Rockets and was now in Europe, was signed. Primus. The roster grew. Interesting? Fun? The tallest player and the shortest player and a player under indictment and everything that heaven allows. There never had been a team like this. On any level.

The league was the invention of a young guy named Dan Meisenheimer from Orange, Connecticut. Meisenheimer, thirty-four, had been the head of an investment advisory firm established by his father. Life was dull. He was making solid investments with solid returns for his clients. Dull. He decided to move along to something more exciting, but he wasn't sure what. He finally formed a new business called Meisenheimer Capital. He promised his investors he would take their money, research inventive schemes, invest in the most likely winners, and everyone would either make a lot of money or lose everything. This was exciting.

In looking for investments, he looked at the possibility of owning a team in the Continental Basketball League. He found that the teams were located mostly in other parts of the country and were mostly low-budget, low-yield operations. Somewhere in the research the idea developed that maybe he could do a better job than the CBA was doing. What if he had his own league . . . what if he sold stock not in a team but in the entire league . . . what if the games were played in . . . the spring?

"This was when the United States Football League was starting up, throwing all that money around," he says. "Remember Donald Trump's face was all over the place? Signing players. Predicting greatness. Challenging the NFL. The USFL was playing football in the spring. I never liked football very much, but I *loved* basketball. If football people would pay money to watch football in the spring, then why wouldn't basketball people like me pay to watch basketball in the spring? It seemed like an unbeatable idea. Why hadn't someone else thought of it first? We stole our name straight from the USFL. The United States Basketball League."

Meisenheimer wasn't exactly Donald Trump, not close, just an ordinary financial guy with a house and family in the suburbs, but these were the eighties. Anything was possible. Money was being made everywhere, banks were handing out loans on cotton-candy illusions, everybody buying, buying, buying. Why wouldn't this work? Basketball in the spring! Catch it!

Meisenheimer initially thought the league would take a year or so of planning, a lot of organizational work at the bottom, but somehow the planning became forgotten. These were the eighties! Now! Instead of waiting a year, he suddenly found himself in December 1984 at a press conference at the Plaza Hotel in New York announcing that the league would start the following spring, in 1985. He was accompanied by former New York Knicks stars Walt Frazier and Earl ("The Pearl") Monroe. Frazier would be the league adviser. Monroe would be the commissioner. Immediate legitimacy! There would be seven teams playing twenty-five-game schedules, followed by playoffs. The players would be whoever was available, recent college graduates, CBA stars, even an NBA type or two who might be looking for some work during the off-season. Was this thing going to fly, or what?

"Looking back, we definitely should have waited another season," Meisenheimer says now. "We really didn't know what we were getting into. Everything happened really fast."

The seven teams were strung along the Northeast. Meisenheimer was the owner of one of them in Springfield, Massachusetts, and was in negotiations with investors to pick up the other six. The general stock plan would be instituted later. His idea attracted mostly other young people like himself, eighties opportunists looking to take a shot. Press conferences were held in the various league cities and towns to announce the formation of the teams and to introduce the owners. In Rhode Island, the owner was a twenty-seven-year-old financial planner from Boston whose father was in the printing business. There were pictures. Everybody smiled for the cameras. The stories ran in the newspapers. Very nice. Then the bills started to arrive.

"All of a sudden, I was having trouble getting through on the phone to this guy who owned the Gulls," Meisenheimer says. "I'd call and he was never in. He was never home. I'd call and call and could never get a hold of him. Finally, I just stopped dialing."

The problem was not unique. Sparing the details, the prospect of spending actual money suddenly scared many investors. Meisenheimer wound up owning four professional sports franchises in the professional sports league of which he was the founder. He became the mogul of moguls. He was still optimistic but getting further and further over his head. He was racing to fulfill a torturous schedule that he had designed for himself.

Strangely, the part of the business he had thought would be hardest—finding players and coaches—turned out to be the easiest. Players appeared from everywhere. Good players. The NBA was a monolith, employing the best 276 players in the world. All the rest of the players who had ever played the game were not only available but willing and able to work. Cheap. One of the few costs Meisenheimer had overestimated rather than underestimated was player salaries. He spent too much too fast for players, accustomed to those big-money figures in the newspaper for the major leagues. The most he spent was for Manute.

"We really wanted Manute," Meisenheimer says. "He'd been

at Bridgeport, about twenty miles away from here, so he wasn't exactly a secret. We knew he would bring us the instant publicity we needed, big as he was. He was one of the first people we contacted. He needed a place to show what he could do. We were perfect for him."

A hasty trade to the Gulls was no problem. The contract was a wrangle. Manute practiced with the Gulls without a contract as Meisenheimer bargained with Catapano. The bargaining continued until a half hour before the first game of the league's history, Rhode Island at Springfield. Catapano said Manute would not take the floor unless the contract was signed. A crowd of over four thousand people had gathered at the Springfield Civic Center, responding to the hype, especially about Manute. What could Meisenheimer do? He signed. Manute would receive $25,000 for twenty-five games, the largest salary then—and, as it turned out, ever—in the league.

"I remember the beginning of that game," Meisenheimer says. "All the people in the seats. Manute. Bingo. This was the way it was going to be forever, only better. I remember thinking that very soon I'd be worth billions and billions of dollars."

His problem was that he didn't know which team to root for when it scored. He owned both of them.

The Gulls lived in a dormitory at Roger Williams College in nearby Bristol, Rhode Island. Stacom wanted them to be freed from the nightlife and temptations of Newport. Each player had his own spartan room. Manute seemed to wind up with Webb much of the time. They were an instant pair. All stories written about Manute and the Gulls showed him pictured with Webb. Long and tall. Mutt and Jeff. Clichéd journalistic perfection. The package was too easy not to resist. All manner of publications came running.

"There was a guy from the *National Enquirer*, pounding on

Manute's door at six in the morning," Stacom says. "The legitimate press came, but that wasn't all. All the supermarket tabloids wanted a piece of this."

"They made such a sideshow out of it," Webb says. "I think that's why, even today, I don't like those size pictures. Okay, I can see it the first time, the big guy and the small guy. Talk about it. But then go on to something else. This didn't stop."

Manute hit the league as a terror. That was one immediate impression. If he only had eight games to prove himself, then they were going to be eight interesting games. He blocked sixteen shots in the opener and went from there. Every night he blocked more shots. Spud was equally exciting. What little man jumped the way he did? John Williams was as advertised, a solid first-round pick. He showed up with his little son and his girlfriend. He was quiet, bothered no one.

Stacom, from the beginning, became a strong Manute backer. He had seen Bill Russell play, the greatest shot blocker of all time. Manute was better. Manute was the greatest shot blocker of all time. Already, Stacom thought Manute had abilities that no one had ever suspected. He was blocking the shots of guys who were a step away from the NBA, some of whom had played in the NBA. He was blocking their shots easily. He was picking up an offensive rebound here and there, strong on the defensive board, leading the team in rebounds, even scoring some points. What more could a coach want for starters?

Still in shape, Stacom would play in some of the scrimmages. He would see, firsthand, the distortions on the court that took place. A fifteen-foot jumper, all alone, no longer was a free and easy shot. A hand would come from someplace and slap it away. Everyone's first impression was that Manute was going to break, that he would simply be snapped in half. Stacom noticed Manute did not break. He did not have to jump very much, tall as he was, so he did not put himself in that much peril. He could simply reach instead of jump. He also seemed to have a grace about him, in his own way. His speed was not bad for his size. He could run

the court all right. He wasn't one of those slow, big-man ca-
booses coming up the floor.

"He was like one of those flamingos," Stacom says. "The first
two steps might look awkward, but once he got moving he was
very graceful."

"My first thought, when I saw him for the first time, was, 'This
is ridiculous,' " Webb says. "How could anybody be so tall? We
became good friends. I think everybody who has ever met Manute likes him and has become his friend. And half of these guys
have had fights with him, too. He has such a good heart. You can
see that. I think he liked me because I was an underdog in a way,
just like him. All of us were underdogs, really. It was like they
thought we should steal something from each other: I should
take some inches from Manute, he should take some ballhandling from me. We all needed something.

"We'd just sit around and talk. Actually, Manute did most of
the talking and we mostly listened. There wasn't much to do in
Rhode Island, so we'd just listen to Manute's stories about hunt-
ing for food with a spear, killing the lion. It was all so far away,
the things he'd had to deal with. We'd been fighting the guns and
the drugs in the ghettos, but he'd been fighting all of this other
stuff. You couldn't believe it."

Webb had never seen anyone block shots the way Manute did.
None of the players had. Not only did he block the shots, but he
kept the ball in play, a trick Russell had perfected. The players
had a tendency to watch in amazement rather than dive for the
ball.

"Manute got really mad about that," Webb says. "He said he
was going to quit because we weren't trying. I had to explain to
him that we'd never seen anything like him. Most guys, they
block a shot, the ball goes right out of bounds. We weren't used
to this. It wasn't that we weren't trying. I had to give him the
Knute Rockne speech. I told him to quit if he wanted, because
that's what the NBA was thinking he was going to do anyway,
that he wasn't tough enough, wouldn't make it. 'Go ahead,' I

said. 'Quit. That's what they expect you to do.' He put his arm around my shoulder. He said, 'Come on, little fella. Let's get back to work.' "

Stacom called Don Nelson, his friend and former teammate with the Celtics, now the coach of the Milwaukee Bucks. He told Nelson to come to Newport because something special was on view. Nelson was interested. He asked Stacom to get some true measurements. Stacom apologized to Manute and asked him to stand still in the locker room. Stacom pulled out a carpenter's tape measure, stood on a ladder and calculated from Manute's feet to the top of his fingers, arms extended. The result was ten feet five inches. Stacom measured Manute's wingspan, side to side, arms lateral. The result was best expressed in furlongs. Stacom sent along a film of a Bridgeport game with his figures.

"It was a Division II game, all these little white kids and this one big man, but I never saw a man do what he did on the film," Nelson says. "He was blocking so many shots, it was like one of those comedy films, like the Keystone Kops. If you've played basketball, you respect all basketball players on all levels for what they do. Here was a guy, blocking fifteen and eighteen shots in a night. That was unheard of. I had to take a look."

Other interest was slight. Dick Motta of the Dallas Mavericks, who had three number one picks in the draft, arrived and did not like what he saw. He said he'd be afraid somebody in the NBA "would hit [Manute] and he'd break like a grasshopper does. An arm here, a leg there." Marty Blake, the NBA's superscout, said, "One of my guys saw him play eleven times at Bridgeport. He can't play a lick." Most teams didn't even bother to look. One team that did was the Washington Bullets.

Bob Ferry, the team's general manager, was mildly intrigued. One of his sons had played college basketball at Harvard with Bruce Webster's son. Ferry called the Bridgeport coach, half hoping Webster would say Manute was a stiff and a trip to Newport was not needed. The opposite happened. Webster asked where the heck everyone had been. This guy was a shot-blocking machine. Wasn't the NBA interested in that sort of stuff anymore? Ferry went to Newport. The first game he saw, Manute blocked sixteen shots. The next game, Manute blocked fifteen. What to make of this?

A jump of the imagination has to be made in scouting any player for the pros, but this seemed to be an Evel Knievel canyon jump. Ferry brought Bullets coach Gene Shue with him. Shue looked at Manute in warm-ups and said, "No chance." Manute blocked his usual dozen or more shots. Shue said, "Well, if he put on some weight and we did some work . . . " What to make of this? The mind could not seem to correlate what the eyes saw.

For Nelson, the more he saw of Manute, the more he liked him. He told reporters that Manute was "the best shot blocker I've ever seen and I played with Russell." He hung around a bit with Manute and Stacom, measuring Manute's personality. He liked Manute's humor and he also liked Manute's desire to succeed. He wondered about Manute's "cultural deficiencies." Could a man come from the jungle and play in the NBA? The Bucks had the twenty-second pick in the draft and Nelson was thinking that he would use it on Manute. Their first pick? He was also thinking that he would not use it, that picking Manute would be a tremendous gamble. Yes? No? What to do?

"I imagine Russell might have done some of the things that Manute can do when he first came into the league," Nelson told *Sports Illustrated*, "but I never saw him block more than five or six shots in a game. This kid is averaging just under thirteen blocks a game. If you called any general manager in the NBA and you told him you had a player who could block ten shots a game if he played forty minutes a night, I guarantee he'd take him, sight unseen. Manute could do that, ten blocks in forty minutes. Of course, you might lose every game because he wouldn't be a factor otherwise."

Draft day came, the last week of June. Manute was leading the Gulls in rebounds, blocked shots, and minutes played. He was averaging thirteen blocks a game. Ferry did not know what to do. Nelson did not know what to do. Stacom thought Dallas, with the three first rounders, also in desperate need of a center, certainly would take a shot. No matter what Motta said. Cleveland seemed to have shown some late interest.

In actuality, Ferry and Nelson were the only bidders. Ferry had the first viable shot, picking twelfth in the first round. Should he? No. He bit his tongue and picked Kenny Green, a forward from Wake Forest. This did not mean Manute was out of the picture. Ferry's plan was to make a trade with Denver, securing Denver's first pick, which was ahead of Milwaukee's pick. He was going to do that until the possibility of a trade with Detroit opened. He sent Rick Mahorn, the player he was going to ship to Denver, to Detroit instead for veteran Dan Roundfield. This killed the Denver deal and Nelson had the open floor. He swallowed his words. A debate had developed in the Bucks' front office. Nelson let himself be talked out of Manute. He picked Jerry Reynolds of LSU.

Ferry finally picked Manute in the second round. Manute was the thirty-first player chosen, the tenth center. Ferry was ecstatic. Not only did he have Manute, he also had Green and Roundfield. A bargain day. Immediate plans were made to ship assistant coach Fred Carter to Newport to help Manute in conditioning and adapting to the Bullets offense. Stacom was disappointed. He had thought Manute would go in the first round, which would have meant much more money for Manute. Stacom was further disappointed about Webb, who wasn't picked until the fourth round by Detroit. Couldn't these NBA people see? Williams, with his court problems still ahead of him, dropped to the second round, picked by Cleveland.

"The Gulls finished third," Stacom says. "We were a young team, remember. There were a couple of teams filled with CBA veterans who knew all the tricks. Springfield, the champion, had

Michael Adams and a lot of CBA guys. We were playing pretty well at the end. The running game was starting to click. If the season had gone longer, and if there'd been playoffs . . ."

The season ended abruptly. All action after the draft almost seemed superfluous. The Gulls were in Wildwood, New Jersey, for a game when Stacom received a call telling him that it would be the last game. One of the many pitfalls Meisenheimer hadn't figured on was that the league schedule ran directly into the time when the NBA started holding rookie camps. Players began leaving teams everywhere, heading for shots as free agents. The league was also losing—had lost and was going to lose—a lot of money. It was time to reassess. End of season. No playoffs.

Stacom saw a certain poetry in the team's spending its final day on the boardwalk of a honky-tonk amusement park. Hadn't this whole experience been a ride on one of those low-budget Tilt-a-Whirls, thrills for a cheap price? The voice on the phone told him not to tell the players. Not tell the players? He told and they played anyway and had some fun and went back to Newport. So much for the Tilt-a-Whirl.

Manute had been as good as advertised, better in fact. Some teams had tried to become physical with him, too physical, and Stacom had brought in Mark Halsel, a six-foot-six power forward he'd known at Northeastern. Halsel had the shaved head and the disposition of middleweight boxer Marvin Hagler. In the first game against one of the New York teams, a couple of players started to bang at Manute. Halsel went into the game and said, "Come on, motherfuckers. You want Manute? You can have him, but you have to come through me." No one came. That was perfect.

The media pressure had started to get to Manute at the end, too many cameras, too many interviews, but Spud had helped. For one game at Westchester, *USA Today* arrived and wanted to do the Spud and Manute picture. Manute would not do it. He was angry, tired. Stacom talked to him. Spud talked to him. Manute did the picture.

"You could see how it could get to him," Stacom says. "It was always the same question, 'Do you think you'll make the NBA?' with the definite implication that 'You may think so, but we don't.' Who wouldn't get sick of that? It always was negative. There's this scene in the movie *The Passenger*. Jack Nicholson is asking this African man these stupid questions. The African won't answer. Nicholson asks why. The African says, 'My friend, your questions reveal more than any answer I could tell you.' That was how it was with Manute."

Stacom organized a farewell party for the team at the Inn at Castle Hill in Newport, one of those bygone mansions, now a restaurant, on a hill overlooking Breton Reef, where the America's Cup boats once raced. He gathered with his odd group on the lawn for a barbecue. He thought about the wacky season, about driving along the beach one day with Manute in the backseat, Bruce Springsteen singing "Born in the USA" on the radio, turned up loud, everybody laughing. There was a toast. Stacom said something about, "Only in America."

"I knew one thing about that team," he says. "I knew that, if nothing else, one day we'd be the answer to a trivia question."

Webb, of course, has had a terrific NBA career, even winning the Slam-Dunk contest. John Williams, acquitted long ago, had the highest salary in the entire league for the 1991–92 season, playing for Cleveland. The USBL has even survived. Meisenheimer tooled down, forgot about billions, and started digging out of the initial hole. He had to close down for one season three years ago, but he came back and had seven teams this year— none that he owned—and he expected the league to finish in the black. The USBL all-star team even played the Soviet—make that Commonwealth of Independent States (CIS)—Olympic team, and he was negotiating about having some of the CIS players in the league in the future. He says he even might form a pro league in the CIS. (The CISBL?) The Gulls, alas, did not survive. They never played another game. Stacom has never coached another game.

"Here's what was strange about Manute," Webb says. "He didn't have a car, didn't drive, but he showed up everywhere. I'd go to eat, suddenly Manute would be in the restaurant. I'd go, say, to an appliance store. There's Manute. He was everywhere. I'd ask him how he got there. He'd just say, 'I have my ways, little fella.' I never figured it out.

"We're still friends. I'll call him up and have to listen to him for about thirty minutes before the conversation will start. He'll go on and on, telling me how I've forgotten about him, how Americans are strange, how they don't keep in touch with their friends, how they only call when they want something. Thirty minutes. Then we can start to talk."

"You know what was great about Manute?" Stacom says. "He had such pride, such guts. He had such a look about him, the look of royalty. He always just stood so tall. Don't you think that's right, Nellie?"

Stacom is having a beer with Nelson in a bar in Boston. This is an annual occasion. Nelson is coaching the Golden State Warriors and whenever they're in Boston he and Stacom meet for breakfast or lunch or dinner or beers. This is the afternoon of the NCAA semifinals. Beers.

"All I know is I should have drafted Manute," Nelson says. "I let someone talk me out of it. I will never do that again with a draft choice."

Eleven years earlier, same type of occasion, another bit of NBA trivia occurred. Stacom, already retired for two years, running the bar in Newport, met Nelson for lunch. Nelson was coaching the Bucks and lamenting the fact that all of his guards were hurt. Where was he ever going to find a guard? He and Stacom went through a few prospective available names. Nelson liked none of them. Suddenly he looked across the table and asked Stacom if he was still playing a little bit at the YMCA or somewhere. Stacom said he was. Nelson asked if Stacom, per chance, had his equipment in the car. Stacom said he did. Nelson brought out a contract. Stacom played that night at the Garden, scored 10 points against the Celtics in a Bucks win and wound up playing fourteen games before Nelson told him to return home. This was stuff that not even Sam Malone would do.

"What do you think?" Nelson is asked. "Another beer. Will you bring out the contract again?"

"Nah," Nelson says. "We have good guards."

He pauses.

"If Kevin were about six feet ten, though," he says, "we might have something going."

The giant moved to Washington, the capital of the Great Outside. He became a star. Sort of a star. He became famous. He became richer than he had ever imagined. He did his tricks and people went crazy. He learned how to drive a car. He married. He broke his nose? He met Mickey Mouse. He went to New Orleans. He traveled everywhere in the Great Outside. He signed his name on strange pieces of paper. Whew.

He did a lot.

Chuck Douglas was twenty-three years old and he was looking for a job in sports marketing. That was what his degree from the University of Maryland said he should be doing. He had put together a nice little résumé for a young guy, working as an intern in his alma mater's sports information office and in the office of the Washington Federals of the USFL and for ProServ, a Washington-based sports agency. He was ready for a real job now and he found one. Almost.

The deal was that he would be employed by the Washington Bullets as a third member of their public relations office. When he left, he could put that fact on his next résumé and he would receive a good recommendation. His actual job was that he would be Manute's manservant.

"It was a job," Douglas says now. "It wasn't exactly what I'd been planning to do with my degree—or my life—right away, but it sounded good. I was on the payroll."

His basic duties were to help Manute, who was suddenly living on his own. Deng was back at Bridgeport, finishing his degree. Deng had been invaluable, an English-speaking voice, a sounding board for the hard times, a bargaining agent in the twentieth-century marketplace. Deng had not gone to Newport, but Manute had been insulated there by his teammates. There would be no more dormitory living, as there had been in Newport, with Spud Webb in the next room, the cast of character actors from the Gulls always hanging around with each other. In the NBA, each player had his own house, apartment, and life-style. This was modern American adult business. Manute's English was fine, but he was moving into a new cultural zone. After two years in America, he could certainly walk and talk, but he was still a little shaky about red lights and green lights and that orange one in the middle.

Douglas was the twenty-four-hour buffer to whatever problems might arise. Manute had lived in a hotel in Maryland from the conclusion of the Gulls season until training camp, going to the University of Maryland daily for a series of tests and exercise sessions. Bob Ferry spent a lot of time with him, and Ferry's son, Danny, later an All-American at Duke and a millionaire with the Cleveland Cavaliers, had been his chauffeur, aide, and confidant. But Ferry now had an entire team to worry about, and his son had to return to Duke. Manute was moving out of the hotel and into an apartment. Douglas was his man.

"Manute had never written a check, driven a car, prepared his own food," Douglas says. "All of the little things you never think about. The truth was, I hadn't done a lot of those things either. I was living with my folks. I was twenty-three. Out of school. I was the wrong man for the job. I hadn't been out much in the adult world myself. The only thing I had going for me was that I had grown up here."

They became a pair. Manute called Douglas "Chief." Douglas owned a 1962 Ford Falcon. Manute sat in the backseat while Douglas drove. Manute called the car "the Train." Manute would sit in the backseat, waiting for Douglas to arrive after practice, and blow the horn without having to stretch. He would shout, "When's the Train going to leave, Chief?" Manute bought an apartment's worth of furniture on one wild $6,000 trip through a furniture store. Douglas signed the check. Manute bought the latest in stereo equipment. Douglas signed. Douglas signed for the gas bill, the electric bill, the water bill, any bill that arrived. Manute had never spent money like this. Neither had Douglas. This was the first experience with money for both of them.

Manute had signed a three-year contract that paid him $130,000 in his first season. The leading edge of the endorsement onslaught was arriving, advertisers waiting to see if he could, indeed, play in the NBA. He eventually wound up as a spokesman for Nike shoes and Church's fried chicken and Kodak cameras and Coca-Cola and assorted local enterprises that paid him another estimated $100,000. The suitcase filled with money had finally arrived. A small suitcase, anyway.

All manner of new experiences awaited. He was on the way.

"I'm signing these checks . . . ," Douglas says. "It's kind of funny now. I'll probably never spend money like that in the rest of my lifetime."

Manute made the team without difficulty. After all the worrying, his spot was almost automatic. Thirteen players were returning from a year earlier, plus first-pick forward Kenny Green from Wake Forest, but there obviously was room for Manute on the twelve-man roster. How could he not make the team after such a grand hoo-ha? A Washington television station, the day Manute was drafted, sent out a reporter with a life-sized cutout of Manute's body. The reporter walked with the cutout into various Washington buildings, the cutout's head scraping ceilings and banging into doorways. The newspapers ran stories on him constantly. Could he? Couldn't he? He was a gate attraction before he even attended one practice session, the most famous backup center in the NBA before he had ever backed up anybody.

"For Manute to succeed to the degree he's capable of, there needs to be a total effort by him and by our organization," Ferry told reporters. "We wouldn't put this much energy into someone who didn't have more than average ability. I know he can help us by doing what he does best, blocking shots and passing the ball. On other things, the challenge is to build up enough strength to play without injuring himself."

He did not disappoint. If anything, he looked much better than he was ever supposed to look. He fit into the operation from the first day. He blocked as many shots in practice as he had ever blocked, swatting and swatting. He was scheduled from the beginning to be a work-as-you-learn backup to often-injured, six-foot-eleven center Jeff Ruland, but now he looked like a backup who could play. Players had to alter their shots, do things differently than they had always done them. There was no difference between NBA players and other players: a seven-foot-seven obstacle is a skyscraper suddenly planted in the middle of a familiar neighborhood. Traffic had to be rerouted. Adjustments had to be made.

His first game as a Bullet was an exhibition against the Boston Celtics in Worcester, Massachusetts. The Celtics, of course, had never seen anyone like him. They stood around during warmups, just taking a look at the other end of the court. He was so tall, so different. He was the only subject of conversation before the game.

"Larry Bird said two things," Bill Walton, who was the Celtics backup at the time, says. "The first was that everybody should watch out. This is this guy's first game. All the cameras are going to be on him. The first time he blocks a shot, that piece of film is going to be shown on every sports show in America. Watch out. This could be embarrassing. The second thing, Larry starts a pool. Everybody has to put up $50. The winner is the guy who dunks first on Manute. There're twelve guys, so the pot is $600. That's a nice little piece of change. Think anybody wanted to dunk on Manute?"

The game was played. Walton entered at the same time as Manute, backup against backup. Walton was wary, but suddenly found himself with an open fifteen-foot jumper, one of his favorite shots of all time. He took it. He wound up on all the sports shows in all the cities in America. Also, no one dunked on Manute. The pot wasn't won.

"He screws up a game more than anybody I've ever seen," Ferry told reporters. "He throws everybody out of synch."

The regular season began and he put up some startling numbers. He blocked fifteen shots against the Atlanta Hawks, second highest total in NBA history. He blocked twelve in a half against the Cavaliers, the players on coach Lenny Wilkens's young team just coming at him, no matter how many shots he threw back. He blocked eleven in a half against Milwaukee. Much of this was as a starter. Starter? An injury to Ruland in December forced Manute into the lineup. In his first game after Ruland's loss, he played forty-eight minutes, scored 18 points, grabbed nine rebounds, and blocked twelve shots against Milwaukee. The Bullets won, 110–108.

He blocked a shot early on Moses Malone in Philadelphia and it seemed to throw the big man into a funk. He blocked a couple of shots on the Chicago Bulls' Jawaan Oldham and Oldham started a fight. That was all right. There was Manute, throwing his lefts and rights from above, getting the best of the brawl. He blocked Kevin McHale's famous fade-away. He did not touch Kareem Abdul-Jabbar's sky hook, but did block a Jabbar dunk.

"It's tough to find him," Abdul-Jabbar said. "Most centers in the NBA lean on you and you know where they are. With him, you have to look around and locate him before you can do anything."

On the team, he was an immediate character. He called forward Tom McMillen, who was preparing to run for Congress, "Tom Congress." He called Ruland "Commando No. 1" and Steve Jones "Commando No. 2." He would shout things in practice like "Jeff Malone—Tastes Great" and "Dudley Bradley—Less Filling." A ball would roll away from him and he would chase it, yelling, "Taxi, Taxi."

"What's the matter?" he would shout at someone whose shot he blocked. "Don't you have a television? You can't do that on Bol."

Anything could happen. He created a different atmosphere wherever he went. On a road trip to New York, he and Ruland went for lunch. They went into a delicatessen. Two Arabs were behind the counter. They began talking Arabic and laughed. There was a pause. Manute suddenly talked in Arabic. The eyes of the two men behind the counter went wide. Manute told Ruland they should go, eat someplace else.

"What happened?" Ruland asked. "What were those guys saying?"

"They said, 'Hey, look at these two tall assholes,' " Manute said.

"What did you say?"

"I said they could bite my dick."

Each city he visited brought a new rush of attention. All of the notebooks and camera crews available were brought to the Bullets' locker room. He was the show. The rush was so great that Mark Pray, the public relations director, had to travel with the team. A press conference was held at each stop, the press and Manute. Manute was not happy about this. The first time around the league was a grind.

"He hadn't grown up in a society that was advertising/promotions-oriented," Pray says. "So he really didn't understand what the fuss was about. I'd tell him there was going to be another press conference and he wouldn't want to do it. Then he'd say, 'Well, okay, but not for them. I'll do it for you.' "

He was a photographer's dream. Which angle shall we use to show how really tall he is? He was even more a writer's dream, an exotic subject in a field of stories that tend toward sameness, great athletes who have always done great things and are now expected to do more great things. The quotes never really moved past the same stories that had been written earlier, but the descriptions were wonderful. Who could not write about seeing this man?

"He's a one-dimensional player with a two-dimensional body and a fourth-dimensional impact," Steve Aschburner of the *Milwaukee Journal* said in his description, which was as good as any. "He is the yin to William ('The Refrigerator') Perry's yang, Bill Veeck's midget hoax put on the rack and left to stretch. He is Wile E. Coyote *after* the steam roller has run over him, Plastic Man on a diet, a CinemaScope movie on a shopping mall screen. He is one of the few persons living—John Madden and Elizabeth Taylor are two others—of whom caricatures seem like photographs."

The publicity crush of the first trip eventually faded a bit. Stories done once did not have to be repeated the second time around, so the media onlookers could move to some other new sensation. The basketball progress also eventually faded. Or leveled off. The one-dimensional aspect of Manute's game seemed to be underlined. He could block shots all night, but could he ever learn to score? If he could score, he could play for substantial amounts of time in a game. If he couldn't, he was destined to be a backup player. How resilient was he? One year down. Could he play another?

This did not mean he hadn't established certain points. There were still questions, but they were so much different now. The major question had been answered: Yes, he could play in the NBA. He had done it. He had done it far better than most people thought he could.

"So we kept the pool going all year with the Celtics," Walton says, a final line to the season. "The equipment man kept the money, the $600. The first guy to dunk on Manute gets it all. The problem is that nobody dunks. The ones who do, it's ruled that Manute wasn't close enough. Something like that. We come to the final game we play against the Bullets at the Cap Centre. It's the third quarter, we're up by a lot. Larry Bird gets a breakaway. He's at half court, nobody around. He stops, still dribbling the ball. He starts calling for Manute, motioning him with one hand. Manute has no idea what's going on, but he runs down to the basket. Larry just starts to fire up. You can see in his eyes, he's going for the dunk of dunks. He dribbles as hard as he can, straight for the basket, Manute in front of him, and as Larry starts to go in the air, he loses the ball. The ball goes flying into the seats.

"We start laughing. Everybody on the floor for us is laughing. Everybody on the bench is laughing. We have tears coming down our eyes. We're out of our seats. The referees look at us like we're crazy. The Bullets look at us like we're crazy. K. C. Jones, our coach, looks at us like we're crazy. We just keep laughing. No one dunked. I think the equipment manager just kept the money."

Domestic life during the season for Manute and Douglas was something out of a situation comedy. Manute lived alone. Douglas still lived with his parents. That did not mean the two men did not see each other often. Manute would call. Douglas would come, any time, day or night. His life was Manute's life. He began to think he was more Manute Bol than Chuck Douglas. Manute bought a town house in the neighborhood around Bowie Community College, where the Bullets practiced. Douglas signed the check. Douglas supervised the move. Manute bought a pool table for the recreation room. Douglas signed the check. Manute stretched the length of the table for those hard-to-reach shots that send most pool players to the side for a bridge. Douglas said this was not fair. They sometimes played with a basketball in the local playground.

"I am going to take you to the ice cream parlor," Manute would say when they played H-O-R-S-E, a game of matching basketball shots.

Huh?

"What flavor do you want, Chief?" Manute would ask as he picked his shot from his strange repertoire.

Some interesting situations developed. Manute told Douglas he wanted to buy "a train." Douglas wondered what a train might be. Manute said it was one of those things that went through the house with a light on the front. Douglas figured that Manute wanted to buy a model train. He took Manute to a giant Toys 'R' Us, to the model trains. Manute said this was not the kind of train he wanted. They wandered the aisles. No trains. They went next to a large department store. Manute finally picked out a large vacuum cleaner. Ah, a train. A light on the front.

"You gotta be the stupidest American I ever met," Manute said. "Take me to a toy store for a train."

Manute said his house had suddenly been filled with animals. He said he needed something to kill them. Douglas suggested an exterminator. Manute said the animals were bothering him because they could fly through the air. Douglas said he never had heard of animals that flew through the air except maybe bats. Manute said he and Douglas should go back to the department store. They went through the aisles again. Manute picked out a can of Raid. The animals were insects.

"I cannot go to practice today, Chief," Manute said sadly on the phone one morning. "I don't feel good. I broke my nose while I was sleeping."

"You broke your nose while you were sleeping?" Douglas asked.

"Only my left nose. My right nose is all right."

"You broke your left nose while you were sleeping?"

"Yes. And there is water coming out."

Douglas figured out the situation. Manute had a cold. He had never had a cold in his life.

Every day was a fine adventure. Manute finally bought a car, a Ford Bronco, with the front seat removed. This was the only way he would ever be able to learn how to drive, to buy the car and have it altered for his legs. Driving lessons and then practice were held around the Capital Centre, where the Bullets played. The building is a big concrete circle located on a stretch of nowhere in Landover, Maryland, midway between Baltimore and Washington. It is surrounded by a field of parking lots. Manute took off. Around and around he went. Faster and faster. Manute liked to drive. Manute liked to drive fast.

"He took Bob Ferry for a ride one day around the building," Douglas says. "He must have been doing ninety. Ferry came out of the car the way you do when you come off a roller coaster at an amusement park. His tie was over his shoulder. His hair was all messed. He looked dizzy."

Early in the relationship, Douglas took Manute to a seamstress. It was time for Manute to be fitted for his first overcoat. The Bullets would play in some cold locales. The seamstress made the patterns, then laid them on the floor. The patterns covered the entire floor. The coat was supposed to be ready in plenty of time for the first cold road trip to Chicago, but the usual complications arrived. Manute was leaving for Chicago on the day the coat would be ready. The temperatures in Chicago were below zero. Manute was worried.

Douglas said there would be no problem. He would pick up the coat at the seamstress, then bring it to the airport before the Bullets boarded the plane. Oops. More delays. Douglas finally received the coat, no time to spare, and started driving as fast as he could. He went through stop signs. He went through red lights. He pulled up in front of Dulles Airport and left the car in a No Parking zone. He started running.

"I came to the security and there was a line," Douglas says. "I'm carrying this coat, which is enormous. The end is dragging on the floor. I just run past security. All the metal detectors go off. People start yelling. I keep running. People start chasing me. I get to the gate and the team is on the plane. I run past the stewardess taking tickets, down the jetway. All these people are chasing me. Manute is sitting in the first seat, first class."

"Manute," Douglas said. "Here's your coat."

Douglas ordered pizza from the pizza restaurants, burgers from the burger restaurants. Douglas bought all the food at the grocery store. The Bullets were worried about Manute's diet. The Dinka tradition is that men do not cook, that it is considered women's work, beneath a man to cook. Manute did not cook. The Bullets would prepare a week's worth of meals for him to put in his refrigerator. He then could put them in his microwave oven at his leisure. That wasn't really cooking, was it?

Everywhere Manute went, Douglas went. He saw the rush of people, the looks on their faces as soon as they saw the big man. *Who is that? Has to be someone.* He saw Manute's moods change as the people continued to assault him. Sometimes he could be friendly, funny. Sometimes he could be distant, almost rude. People would say the weirdest things, ask him to stand up so they could see how tall he really was. "Can't," Manute would say. "My leg's broken." People would ask how the weather was up there. "I am not Bob Ryan," Manute would say, naming the local TV weatherman. People would ask if he played basketball. "Football," Manute would say. "Quarterback. Washington Redskins."

"He had a great sense of figuring out who was real and who wasn't," Douglas says. "He could tell the people who were making fun of him, the ones who were just interested in him because he was so tall. He could tell the people who were being truly friendly. And he didn't give anyone the benefit of the doubt. He made his decisions. That was that. The group of friends he made ... I realized one day that if Manute were in some kind of trouble he could call on ten times as many friends as I had. And I'd lived in the area all my life."

One of the trips during the season was to New York. Manute was booked for the first time on "Late Night with David Letterman." Douglas went with him. Douglas was worried; he had seen Letterman's show. Letterman liked to make fun of his guests. Douglas warned Manute. He told him Letterman would try to cut him up.

"Don't worry, Chief," Manute said. "I'll kill him."

Manute even had a joke planned for Letterman. He would say, "Your name is Letterman. Do you enjoy delivering mail?" He asked Douglas what he thought of the joke. Douglas said it was awful. Manute said he was still going to use it.

The show turned out to be a reserved affair. Letterman didn't cut up Manute and Manute did not kill him. Letterman truly seemed intimidated by someone this large. The conversation covered the usual topics of killing the lion and losing the teeth during the initiation ceremony. Manute said he now had money enough to buy a lot of teeth. There was no time for Manute's joke. It never fit. When the show was finished, Manute and Douglas returned to the hotel and stopped at the bar. Douglas began a conversation with the woman bartender. He liked her and she seemed to like him. He felt pretty good about himself. They talked for a while. Then he suddenly remembered Manute. Where was Manute? Douglas turned and searched the bar. Manute was sitting in a booth with three women. Douglas had been feeling good about his conversation with one woman and Manute was talking with three women. Manute waved.

"Someday you'll learn, Chief," he said.

*   *   *

At the end of the season, the Bullets asked Manute to go to New Orleans. They were concerned about his weight. He weighed 195 pounds, and even though he had survived quite well, there still was the idea that he might be hit once and simply break apart. If he was as good as he was at 195, what would he be like if he added some bulk to help him stand inside against those brutes the size of Moses Malone? A nutritionist and weight guru named Mackie Shilstone from New Orleans had gained a lot of publicity by building up boxer Michael Spinks, adding twenty-five pounds to a light heavyweight frame to make a heavyweight champion. Ferry had read about Shilstone in *Sports Illustrated*. He figured Shilstone might be an answer. Manute went to New Orleans for six weeks.

"The Bullets asked me how I wanted to get paid," Shilstone says. "I said, 'Pay me by the pound.' It was the best deal I ever made. They thought I was crazy. I wound up making between $12,000 and $15,000. We got Manute a room at the Bayou Plaza. We brought in a big bed and had the shower head raised. We went to work."

The first thing Shilstone did was run Manute through a series of medical tests. His first worry was that Manute might have Marfan's syndrome, a disease that eventually kills some extremely tall people. The big part of that examination is a CAT scan. Shilstone assured Manute that there would be no pain, that everything would be fine. Manute was stretched out for the test. He called Shilstone "Mack Man." A nurse said they now would inject some dye, so they would be able to see various features in an X-ray.

"Die?" Manute said. "I don't want to die, Mack Man."

"I found, early, that he had a tendency to take everything very literal," Shilstone says. "My wife would say something . . . oh, 'It's raining cats and dogs.' Manute would say, 'It's not raining cats and dogs.'"

There were no signs of disease. Shilstone's observation was that Manute was malnourished. He was no different from a lot of young athletes; left on his own, he was eating a constant junk-food diet. The seven salads a week the Bullets were giving him were not being touched. He wasn't even putting them in the refrigerator. Shilstone asked why Manute wasn't eating the salads. Manute said he didn't want to eat those little crawly things inside. What little crawly things?

"There were cockroaches in the salads," Shilstone says. "He was just leaving the food out like that."

Shilstone put him on an exercise program, plus a diet that included three meals and eleven supplements a day, vitamin drinks mixed with apple juice, which Manute liked. This was a virtual high-tech return to the *toc,* the milk-drinking orgy of Manute's youth. He was being bombarded with calories. Shilstone said it was like "having an IV, without the IV." The results came. In six weeks, Manute gained thirty-eight pounds. He could never get up to the 280 or 290 that some dreamers might think would be reasonable, but 228 was possible. Shilstone found that Manute had fine control of his body for a man that size, that he was extraordinarily supple, that he would bend and not break. Manute was resilient. He also was innately strong.

"I've worked with four hundred athletes now," Shilstone says, "but I have to say Manute was unique. I remember we used to play basketball, two-on-two, in the afternoons. My challenge was to get two points off Manute. He said I'd never do it. Near the end, I scored two points. I dribbled the ball between his legs. That's how I got by him. I scored the basket. Two points. He said, 'You cheat, Mack Man.' I said, 'Get out of here, you big drink of water.' "

To keep Manute company in New Orleans, the Bullets had sent along six-foot-nine Jay Murphy, a free agent from Boston College whose agent was Frank Catapano. Murphy, who had a slender frame, though not as slender as Manute, also went through the workouts and took the supplements. He also added bulk and strength. He went to training camp from New Orleans and surprised everyone. He made the team.

*   *   *

The new weight, alas, was not enough weight. Not enough to play forty minutes of every game, clearing out territory beneath the basket, making two-handed dunks and scoring a lot of points. That was the Bullets' evaluation when they brought Manute back for the new season. They had dealt the injured Ruland to Philadelphia for Moses Malone, the bulky epitome of inside basketball, six feet ten, 255 pounds of hard business. Malone would be the starter, the bruiser. Manute would be the surprise change of pace. He would always be spindly, the exaggerated overgrown newborn colt. He said that he felt too slow already with the weight he had added with Shilstone. He could never put on fifty, sixty, seventy pounds no matter how tall he was. His body was his body. His style was his style. He was what he was.

"If he could truly bulk up, there's no limit to what he could do," Kevin Loughery, the Bullets coach that year, now says. "Unfortunately, he could never do that. He doesn't have the ability to put on weight. If he had the strength, he could establish himself underneath. He just doesn't have it. He has a surprising feel for the game, coming to it so late. He's a very good passer. You see him in practice, he's dribbling behind his back, he's not a bad outside shooter. He just doesn't have the strength to play offense once the game starts."

Loughery had become the coach at the tag end of the previous season. He basically saw Manute as a defensive specialist brought into the game to help create mayhem. The Bullets guards would press and trap and run all over on defense, knowing they had Manute in the background to swat away the lay-ups that might result. Manute had started sixty games as a rookie. He started twelve in his second season. He had scored 3.7 points per game as a rookie. He now averaged 3.1. His minutes were less. His total rebounds and blocked shots were less. The limits on his career somehow were established: He was not going to be the new Russell or Abdul-Jabbar. He was going to be a tall character actor, not a leading man.

"This isn't to downplay what he does," Loughery says. "There's never been anyone like him in the NBA, a guy who can come off the bench and change a game defensively. He can do that. He can turn a game around, coming off the bench, can win the game for you with his defense. Who else could do that? He was very effective for us in that role."

The words were still the same from Manute when he was on the court. The confidence was still the same. There still were some laughs. An encounter with John Salley, then a rookie with the Pistons from Georgia Tech, was typical. Salley, seeing Manute for the first time, thought he was seeing "a tree without leaves." The tree without leaves suddenly spoke. The tree said, "John Salley, I have been watching you in college. You are my favorite player."

"This was during warm-ups," Salley says. "I was flattered, to tell the truth. This man I didn't know had seen me and appreciated my talent. I liked that. Then, the game was played. I think Manute blocked four of my shots in a row. I got pissed. I drive to the basket, elbow him hard in the ribs, and make a lay-up. We go down to the other end of the court. Manute comes over and says to me, 'John Salley, that was not nice. I don't think you are my favorite player anymore.' I started laughing."

The Bullets team was not very good, finishing 42–40, bounced from the playoffs in three games by the Detroit Pistons. Loughery says there were a lot more problems than Manute. The team simply did not have much talent.

At the end of this season, Manute returned to Khartoum. He had a purpose. He wanted to find a bride. Female companionship had never been a problem in the United States; women were charmed by Manute. Indeed, they were fascinated by him. Bruce

Webster, back at Bridgeport, had noticed how many women would ask him about Manute. Women of all ages, races, social status, heights, and weights were interested. Webster says he was one of the few people in America who believed Wilt Chamberlain when he wrote in his autobiography that he had made love to twenty thousand different women. Women seemed to be fascinated by huge men. If women were attracted so much to Manute by his size, back when he was so new to the country, still being fitted for teeth, what would someone like Chamberlain, smooth and urbane and living on the top of a Los Angeles hill in a mansion with a circular bed, do with that interest?

Manute did not fully return the interest. He had dates and relationships, but he never fell in love with American women. He found them to be very different from the women of the Sudan, far too independent for his taste, too quick with their opinions. A woman was not only supposed to stand by her man, but step a few paces back, too. Women's liberation is not a cause that has gained great popularity in Africa and the Middle East. A woman is supposed to stay in the kitchen, to raise the children, to be available to her man. She is not supposed to offer her opinions.

"We'd take Manute out to eat in New Orleans every Saturday night," Shilstone says. "It was a treat at the end of a week. Because he is so big, we rented a limousine. My wife and I and Manute would go to a restaurant for blackened baby ribs, which he really liked. We did this for four straight weeks. Rented the limo. Went to the restaurant. On the fourth Saturday, we're driving around the city and my wife is talking about points of interest. She is describing the different buildings, telling the history behind them. Tourist stuff. Manute suddenly says, 'Do you know the problem with you American women? You talk too much.' My wife just wanted to kill him."

Manute wanted a traditional Dinka wife through a traditional, arranged marriage. He'd tried to be married once, earlier in his life, before he had ever come to the United States. A girl named

Nyanhial, a sister of one of his Dinka friends, had drawn his attention when he was living at the Catholic Club in Khartoum. He had initiated a quiet courtship, having friends talk to her about him, send her letters about him. He finally talked to her himself. He told her he wanted to go out with her. She agreed. He soon proposed. She accepted.

At first they decided to elope, which is permissible by Dinka custom. They even went away together for a day. Then Manute decided that rather than alienate her family, they would work for a traditional, arranged marriage. This involved the payment of cows by Manute's father to Nyanhial's father. A sort of kickback was also part of the deal, Nyanhial's father giving Manute's father a certain number of cows in return, say two cows for every ten received. A meeting was held, back in the south, between the fathers and a group of Bol elders. Manute's father balked. He decided that Nyanhial's family was not wealthy enough for Manute, did not own enough cows. Manute argued. He threatened to leave the family forever, a serious threat. Manute's father begrudgingly offered thirty-five cows. Nyanhial's father demanded fifty cows. A woman's status in Dinka society is determined in part by how many cows she fetches in marriage. *See that one? Her husband's father paid sixty cows for her.* No agreement could be reached. The marriage fell apart.

"I was hurt, really," Manute said to Blaine Harden of *The Washington Post,* to whom he described all of this business. "It bust me up."

Manute, his father dead, was now the master of his own deal. He would do the negotiating with his prospective bride's father. He had a female cousin in Khartoum search for a mate. She sounded out different women, many of them leery of marrying someone so tall and who now lived so far away. Eventually, though, she found an eighteen-year-old girl named Atong who seemed interested. Atong was a refugee in Khartoum, coming from the area near Manute's village. Manute's father had known Atong's father. There was a connection. Manute entered into negotiations, settling on the sum of eighty cows, thirty-five now with the rest to arrive at the conclusion of the war. Manute was in Khartoum for two months, settling all of these affairs. He left as a married man.

"I picked Atong and him up at the airport," Chuck Douglas says. "It was an unbelievable scene. She was still wearing these clothes from the wedding ceremony, these robes, and she still had this paint all over her face. I guess that was part of the ceremony, too. You have to leave the paint on your face for a few days. Everyone in the whole airport just stopped and looked. It was such an exotic sight."

Finally, Manute's domestic problems were solved. He would eat well again, eat the foods he liked. He could eat the meals of his youth, if he wanted, cooked by a Dinka woman. He was back on a more traditional course, a family man, with a wife and a first baby, a girl, who arrived before the next season was finished. This was what he had always wanted. Atong knew no English and was at the same cultural level as Manute had been when he arrived. He was now the teacher about America and she was the student.

"Some of us took Manute and his bride out for lunch a few days after they arrived," Susan O'Malley, now president of the Bullets, says. "We went some place, maybe six or eight of us, sitting around a big table. Manute's wife was very pretty, but she couldn't say much because of the language. The waiter came and most of us ordered sandwiches. Manute ordered steaks for his wife and himself. When the meal came, we all picked up our sandwiches and began to eat . . . and Atong looked at us and picked up her steak. Manute said something real stern in Dinka. She put the steak down and began to use the silverware. You could see that she was going to have to go through the same things he had gone through, just to adjust."

*   *   *

The third season was Manute's last in Washington. He says he knew he was doomed from the moment Loughery was replaced as coach by former Bullet Wes Unseld midway through the schedule. Manute did not like Unseld and Unseld did not like Manute. As a player, Unseld had been the opposite of Manute, an inside pounder, a wide man with a big-butt center of gravity, able to capitalize on all the skinny bodies in the neighborhood of the basket, though never bodies as skinny as Manute's. As a broadcaster, prior to becoming coach, he had also traveled with Manute. They were not friends.

"I remember we were taking the bus back from a game in New Jersey," Manute says. "We were sitting near each other, talking about black Americans and Africans in America. He didn't like the things I was saying. I didn't like the things he was saying. We did not get along after that. Then, he becomes the coach . . . he says to me, 'I got your ass now.' "

Manute could not be the physical type of player Unseld had been. He says Unseld would yell at him all the time, asking him, "You want to play?" He says Unseld would blame him for strategic mistakes. Manute says he would argue that he did not make the mistakes. He says there was an actual fight in the locker room in Chicago after a loss, a claim Bullets officials deny.

"He yells at me and I turn around and punch him," Manute says. "We have a fight. I don't care how big he is. You can be big, but I don't have to be afraid. I will fight anyone."

The season was another lackluster march to an early playoff end, though the record did improve after Unseld became coach. Manute again played fewer minutes, scoring fewer points and averaging lower numbers in all categories. When he was traded on June 8, 1988, to the Golden State Warriors for reserve center Dave Feitl and a second-round draft pick, it was a relief. The Bullets' confidence in Manute had fallen. He was going to a place where his friend, Don Nelson, was the coach. Things could not have worked out better, except he now had to move to another coast and another environment.

"It was all part of rebuilding," Bob Ferry says about the trade. "I don't think we ever felt Manute was going to be a starting center and there were questions about his durability. He was still so slight of build. Our doctors worried that if he ever twisted a knee, he'd be done. And Nelson wanted him badly."

Ferry was heartened most at the growth of Manute in other areas. Had any other NBA team worked so hard with one player on so many off-court problems, problems that couldn't even be anticipated? Would any other team in the future have to work so hard? Manute had learned how to drive and eat and dress and spend money and . . . how many other things had he learned? He had learned a culture, while playing in the biggest basketball league of all. The word Ferry uses is "fearless." Manute was fearless in many things.

"Here's how he had grown," former public relations director Pray says. "When the trade came, Manute knew there would be a lot of interest. He invited all the television stations, all the best reporters to his home. He did all the interviews. He served refreshments. This was someone who hated doing all of that stuff. He was gracious. You could see how much his comfort zone had grown."

There was a celebration a month later, however, with friends in Washington about the trade. The celebration went late. At 5:30 in the morning, Manute was stopped by the Maryland state police for failing to yield to a fire truck. He agreed to a Breathalyzer test, failed, and the police went to handcuff him. He refused. A scuffle began and three state troopers finally toppled him to the ground. He was arrested for drunken driving, resisting arrest, and assault. A second arrest for drunken driving came five weeks later, also in Maryland, but without any scuffle. He refused to take the Breathalyzer test on the advice of Frank Catapano.

"You know what I've always maintained?" Pray says. "I think it was the driving part, not the drinking part that got him in trouble. I've been out with him. Those long legs can absorb a lot of beer. I never saw him out of line. The driving, though, he was a terrible driver. Those were two moving violations."

"He had to adjust to a different life," Chuck Douglas says. "He was married now, on his own. He had to drive himself around. This was learning. He couldn't go out with his friends, drink beer, then be driven home. He learned. This was serious stuff. He was on his own."

Douglas's job as manservant was only supposed to last for one season. Even by the middle of that season, he could tell that Manute was needing him less and less. The way things go sometimes in the world of business, though, he had put himself in a good position. Douglas had shown that he was a solid citizen, a punctual employee. He certainly could bring an overcoat to the airport on time. The Bullets looked for something else for him to do. Ferry asked him to start reviewing films of coming Bullets opponents, finding strengths and weaknesses and patterns on offense and defense. Douglas had no experience in this, but Ferry showed him what he should be looking to see. Douglas followed the instructions and soon found himself doing more and more films, even less with Manute. Eventually Ferry started asking Douglas to go to small-college games to judge possible draft choices. Douglas went.

Seven years have passed, and he is still working. He is a Bullets assistant coach and scout. How many basketball men throughout the country hunger for a job on an NBA bench and never come close? Douglas never even wanted it. He wanted to sell the product, not be part of it. Manute changed everything. Manute changed his life.

"I learned so much from that experience," Douglas says. "About everything. About people. About Manute. He has such an inner strength. That is what I admire about him the most. To do what he did? How well would any of us survive in the environment where he came from?"

In the summer of Manute's second season, before he went to New Orleans, he was offered a free trip by the people at Disney World in Orlando. They were thinking of creating a special room in one of their luxury hotels, a Manute Bol Suite. They asked him if he could come to the park to talk. He was allowed to bring two people. One of the people was Douglas.

They stayed in the Michael Jackson Suite. They had unlimited run of the park. They did all the rides. Manute inside Space Mountain. Manute riding the teacups. Manute in the gondolas high above the crowd. Douglas remembers that as they walked from ride to ride, people would stop and stare, as they always did, but somehow it fit. Manute was another happy attraction. He made people feel good. He was in there with Goofy and Snow White and all the Seven Dwarfs and Mickey and Donald. It said something. Manute was seen with that same sense of wonder as the other fantasy figures. From the beginning, people immediately liked him. The other big men of basketball have mostly been cast as sinister characters, booed wherever they went as brutes who manhandle smaller, more respectable people. The reaction to Manute was never like that. He was a joy from the beginning. People smiled. Douglas remembers two elderly women at Disney World who saw him and stopped, spellbound.

"There he is, Hazel," the first one said.

"Who?"

"Him."

"Who?"

"There. You know who he is."

"Who?"

"It's . . . it's . . . Too Tall Sampson."

The giant found that life sometimes could be complicated, even in the Great Outside. As soon as he would begin to feel settled, performing his tricks, living in his new house, someone would ask him to move. Where? He had to move all the way across The Great Outside to a place called California. California? The giant moved and found a place to live and made friends and suddenly he was told he had to move again. Again? Where? Back across The Great Outside. To Philadelphia.

This all was very confusing to the giant, but he went. He could handle anything. He was a giant.

He simply made more friends . . .

The people are always waiting outside the Ambassador Hotel in Barcelona. Pilgrims. Fans. In the morning, there might be only seven or eight of them, maybe a dozen, standing behind the iron police barricades, staring across the street at the three armed guards in front of the double glass doors. In the late afternoon, early evening, there might be five hundred, six hundred, maybe a thousand. A mob. Everyone is waiting for a glimpse of the players on the U.S. basketball team at the 1992 Summer Olympics. The Dream Team.

Has any athletic team anywhere ever had such around-the-clock adulation? Two helicopters fly above the luxury bus from the luxury hotel to the arena for all games. Sirens on policemen's motorcycles scream. Clear a path. Coming through. This is the ultimate extension of celebrity, basketball players who have become as idolized as rock stars. Chris Mullin is a prominent part of the band.

"Are you going to work out today?" an NBA official asks in the lobby of the hotel.

"Sure," Mullin says.

"Do you think it will be soon?" the official asks. "Arnold Schwarzenegger is already at the gym. He's waiting."

Mullin is twenty-nine years old, six feet seven, 215 pounds. He is at the top of his profession, a superstar forward for the Golden State Warriors. As part of this team—the eleven best players from the NBA plus college player of the year Christian Laettner—he is part of basketball history. Never has a more dominant all-star team been put together in any sport. The idea is to send a message to the rest of the world that American basketball is still the best basketball. The games have been a succession of ridiculous blowouts.

"It's been an amazing experience," Mullin says, "just being part of this."

Walking through the lobby are the other stars. Here is Magic Johnson, holding his baby on his shoulder, telling Mullin to give a good interview. There is Karl Malone, the Mailman, dressed for a workout. Larry Bird was here a minute ago. Michael Jordan. Here is Patrick Ewing. He is also ready for a workout. Does Mullin know that Arnold Schwarzennegger is waiting? Every player has a $900-per-day suite of rooms. The only residents in the hotel are NBA players and staff and their families. A perpetual buffet seems to be in operation. It includes chicken every day because Magic likes chicken.

A function room has been converted into a giant game room and nursery, video games everywhere, plus a pool table and a giant-screen television with an up-to-date video library. All amenities have been taken of, all needs fulfilled. The entire hotel was redecorated just in time to house this team. Training camp was held in Monaco. Monaco! The flight from the United States was on a fat charter aircraft, as comfortable as a sultan's living room.

"What is there not to like?" Mullin asks.

He has taken the entire experience seriously. There are reports that other all stars have used it mostly as a vacation, shadow-walking through the practices, exploding only for the games. He has gone to all of the practices, played them as hard as he could. He has kept to his regular high-tech workout schedule after and before the practices, working on the strength and endurance machines. Playing on this team is an honor. He can think of only one greater honor he has encountered in all of basketball.

"Do you know what that is?" he asks. "When Manute named his first child after me. No kidding. Of all the things that have happened to me in this game—all the awards, even playing here—that meant as much as anything to me. He didn't even tell me he was going to do it. He just did it. Someone else, in fact, told me about it. I was as touched by that as I was by anything."

Chris Mullin is Manute's friend.

They probably form the strangest couple in the game. If Manute is the blackest of all the black players in a predominantly black league, Mullin is the whitest. With his burr-head crewcut and his Irish-American, never-tan skin, he is almost a character from another basketball time, a Fifties child who has stumbled into a space-age extravaganza and has still been able to flourish. His accent is 100 percent Brooklyn, his face from a documentary about the troubles in Belfast. Manute's nickname for him is sometimes "Irish." At other times, the nickname is "Chalk." Then again, the nickname is anything at all.

"I'll bet he's had a hundred of them," Mullin says. "And you know what? I always know he's talking to me. I answer to all of them."

Mullin's younger brother, John, played with Manute at Bridgeport. That was where the friendship began. John Mullin was a freshman while Manute was a freshman and sometimes, on weekends, John Mullin would take Manute home. Chris was playing in his senior season at St. John's in Queens, already an All-American, a certified No. 1 draft choice, playing in the Big East, the biggest of college basketball's big time. John Mullin and Manute would go to the games at Alumni Hall, Manute causing a stir as he walked into the gym. Everyone would go back to Brooklyn after the games to celebrate.

"Manute really seemed to like my family," Chris says. "I guess it's because we had a big family and he came from a big family. He just fit in. My father loved him. He'd tell his stories. He'd talk about fighting a gorilla. Really. Fighting with a gorilla. He'd say, 'You have trouble when you fight a gorilla. Those gorillas are strong. A gorilla will kick your ass.' I'd say, 'Gee, here's this guy talking about fighting a gorilla, while I've been trying to keep from being run over by a cab.' It was all so interesting. I loved to hear him talk."

Chris would go to Bridgeport sometimes to work out. Manute would work out at St. John's. There was a mutual love of action, of games. Manute would play any game at any time. Play some H-O-R-S-E? Sure. Some one-on-one? Fine. Pool? Pinball? "I am the best. You cannot beat me." Mullin gladly supplied the competition. Manute often stayed overnight in Brooklyn, sometimes sleeping in a brother's empty bed, sometimes sleeping on a string of pillows laid across the living room floor, his feet sticking out a door. Everything was light and easy. They would travel to the Irish taverns on Flatbush Avenue, all the drinkers stopping in the middle of their conversations when the group walked in. John

Mullin was part of the picture. Manute soon referred to him as "Chris Mullin's brother." Another perfect nickname. Wasn't that what the newspapers always called him? Chris Mullin's brother.

"It was a lot of fun," Chris says. "Then I graduated and was drafted by Golden State. Manute went to Washington. I'd see him when we played the Bullets and we'd go out, but that was it. That was three years. Then he was traded to the Warriors. That was when we really hit it off. I just enjoyed being around him so much."

What could be better than having a friend already in place? Manute arrived with his growing family and settled into a house in Alameda that was only a block from Mullin's house. Friends and neighbors. They could travel to practice together. They could eat lunch together. They could simply talk. Mullin found that he would take his dog for a walk, travel past Manute's house and decide to stop, just to say hello. Two hours later, maybe three, he would leave. There always would be some activity in Manute's house, some African visitors. Mullin would sit and listen to stories about places and situations he had never considered. He loved to listen to Manute talk.

"His ideas, the way he'd say things," Mullin says. "I could listen all day. The way he takes everything literally. He'd make me laugh."

One of the constant visitors was Akuei Mawal, Edward Bona's brother, another of Manute's cousins. Mawal actually lived in the house for the first few months, helping Manute adjust to this new environment. Mawal had been living in San Francisco for three years. He knew the adjustments that were needed. Dinkas in California were a rare sight.

"There were only two other Dinka families in the entire Bay area," he says. "One at UC-Davis, another in San Jose. Actually, that was sort of a problem. Not so much for Manute, but for his wife. Atong really missed the company of Sudanese women. It was very hard for her. She was making the same shortcut Manute made, but it was much harder for her. She was so young. I could take her out, but I couldn't be in the same company a woman would be. Chris's girlfriend helped and Chris's family, but Atong still had to be lonely. Just to talk to Sudanese women."

Mullin's girlfriend—now his wife—helped Atong find a playpen. There were two babies now, Abouk and Madut, and a playpen was a necessity. Didn't they have playpens in the Sudan? Apparently not. Now Atong could place the children in a controlled environment and be free to do other things around the house. What about a stroller? A stroller was purchased. Now Atong could take a walk with the two children.

There was a pleasant sense of shared adventure. Mullin and his girlfriend arrived on Halloween night with a costume for Abouk. They dressed her as a kitten, painting whiskers on her face. They led her into the neighborhood. Halloween? This was something new.

"She was just so shy," Mullin says, "but we pushed her in there with the other kids in the neighborhood. She went to a door and got the candy. Pretty soon she was running up to the doors. She was having so much fun."

Mawal coincidentally had lived in Washington during Manute's first year as a Bullet. He was able to judge how much his cousin had grown in three years of NBA living. He was pleased. In Washington, he had offered to show Manute the city, take him to the famous buildings and monuments. Manute wanted no part of it. Here, Manute wanted to see everything. They went to the Golden Gate Bridge and the Coit Tower and rode the cablecars and hit all the spots on the tourist map. Mawal noticed that his cousin was dressing better, copying the wardrobes of other NBA players, and was far more at ease with the bits and pieces of modern American life. Everything seemed to work.

"Chris was very good for Manute," Mawal says. "He's one of the nicest people I've met in America. He's very polite. A lot of Americans, they bombard you with questions. Chris is not like that. He's not just finding out what he wants to know and then moving on. He sits down and socializes."

There was another bond between the two men. Mullin was coming back from alcohol abuse problems that had caused him to miss twenty-two games during the past season while he was in a rehabilitation program. He was sober and committed to a workout schedule that would make him a superstar within a year. Manute was coming off the two drinking and driving violations in Maryland, plus his troubles with Unseld. He was committed to proving himself again in the league. He wasn't joining any Alcoholics Anonymous program and he wasn't going on any exercise schedule that was even close to what Mullin followed, but he was an ever-present confidant and partner. He was Mullin's roommate on the road.

"We'd play any kind of game that was available," Mullin says. "Pool? Anything. We'd wrestle. We'd have wrestling matches, me against him. We'd always play basketball. The day of the game? We'd play one-on-one against each other at the shootaround. Forty-five minutes. Hard. I like to get up a good sweat and Manute just loves to play. The games would be really competitive. Maybe I'd win six, but Manute would win the seventh. He'd win his share. He always played hard."

This was fun. The friends were back together. And they were playing for Don Nelson. This was a lot of fun.

"You can never overestimate what Manute did for us," Nelson says. "He brought our franchise from a negative to a positive. People were really down on the Warriors. He made them fun again. We sell out every game now and he helped start that as much as anyone."

Nelson was back at the sideline for the 1988–89 season after a one-year stretch as general manager. He looked as if he had gone to a Tibetan retreat and returned as a basketball genius. Walking the sidelines with his hair flopping in his eyes, his suitcoat flying, he yelled instructions and did strange pirouettes when officials made bad calls, and he coached a team that won twenty-three more games than it had a year earlier. Mullin was spectacular, freed from his alcohol troubles. Mitch Richmond, a top draft choice, was immediate help. A number of lesser names helped the team fly. The Warriors were as exciting to watch as any team in the NBA.

Manute was Manute. He came off the bench at strategic spots. He led the league in blocked shots. He brought a buzz to a crowd that had not buzzed often. The Manute Bol Growth Chart became a big seller in the concession stands. He became the team's most requested speaker. A seven-game ticket package was named after him.

A significant addition to his repertoire was the three-point shot. Nelson's teams historically had played what he called "isolation" with their big men who were not very strong offensively. The idea was that the Warriors' big man would stand at the top of the faraway three-point circle. The opposition big man, according to the rules, would have to come away from the basket to guard him. The Warriors' smaller players would then have an easier, less-encumbered route to the basket. Manute, with his bad hands and offensive shortcomings, was a perfect choice for isolation.

"The thing about it is, though, that it isn't very inspiring," Nelson says. "The big man doesn't have much to do. We wanted to give Manute something else, to make him feel more involved. I'd watched him shooting in practice and he wasn't bad . . ."

The Manute three-pointer. It became the most ungainly, but probably most popular, shot ever seen in all of the NBA. Here was this giant man who could reach the basket with his hands if he simply stood close enough, standing instead as far away as possible. The man guarding him would cheat backward, trying to help other people on defense. The ball would suddenly come to Manute. He would look at it as if it had been dropped from the sky. What to do? "Shooooooooot," the crowd would shout. He would pull his right hand and the ball back to the side of his head, forming a sort of catapult. Shooooooooot. He would shoot with the casual ease of someone taking a last shot in the driveway before dinner, halfway walking to the back door. The ball . . . would . . . go . . . in?

He hit the first three-pointer of his career twenty games into the season and was on the way. He became, okay, a bit three-point crazy. For a while it was fine. He took seventy shots. He hit nineteen. Then the slump arrived. He went 1-for-21 to end the regular season. He went 2-for-22 as the Warriors were bounced from the playoffs in five games.

"It was a change, all right," Nelson says. "It went from everyone yelling 'Go, Nute, Go,' to 'No, Nute, No.' We calmed him down the next year."

The next year was another rise for the Warriors. They added rookie guard Tim Hardaway, the Lithuanian star Sarunas Marciulionas and the German Uwe Blab. The looked a little like a United Nations peace-keeping force. Ralph Sampson, the seven-foot-four former college sensation, was also part of the package. Ralph and Manute made almost fifteen feet of slim centers before Ralph was traded to Sacramento. Manute beat him out. Simple as that. Bruce Webster at Bridgeport had once tried to find out what plays and training techniques had been used at Virginia for the fabled Sampson. Manute now beat out Sampson for a job. Heady stuff.

In the off-season, a new contract arrived. Manute was working on an escalating deal that would total $4.2 million for four years. More heady stuff. He had received $130,000 in salary in his first year in Washington. He really was in the NBA now. He was in that millionaire world. This was the far end of the dream from long, long ago. He was where he always wanted to be.

"I'm in Houston on a business deal, I go to see him play," John O'Reilly, the guard from the Bridgeport days, says. "We go out after the game. When Manute came to Bridgeport, I was wearing number ten. Manute said he wanted it. I didn't care, so I gave it to him. Now he still is wearing number ten with the Warriors, but he says Hardaway wants it. He says he's told Hardaway he can have it for $15,000. Can you believe it? I say, 'Hey, wait a minute. I gave you that number for nothing. Now you can get $15,000? What do I get?' Manute turns to the waitress. He says, 'Get this man a beer on me.' "

"I go see him after a game in Boston," Mark Farisi, another Bridgeport friend, says. "We're in a place. Marvin Hagler, the former middleweight champion, comes in. All he wants to do is meet Manute. I'm from Boston and Marvin Hagler's my all-time idol. And here he is. He won't leave Manute. You know what Manute does all night? He rubs Marvin Hagler's bald head. All night. Marvin Hagler's head."

The down side did not arrive until the end of the season. Manute had partially torn a knee cartilage in February, not enough for surgery but enough to slow him down. The Warriors suddenly had the same worries the Bullets had. What if he falls apart? Lynam, still thinking about that big X to put on a paper to fight those opposing Os, arrived from Philadelphia with a proposition. He would give the Warriors a first-round draft choice at the end of next season for Manute. Nelson accepted the offer.

Manute, who was in Egypt when the trade was announced, said he was angry. He had heard rumors of a trade and Nelson had told him not to worry. Nelson said he was sorry, but business was business. The deal was too good. This did not mean he was not Manute's friend. A fan named Matt Moran was quoted in the *Oakland Tribune* as saying that Manute "humanized the team." The fan also said he liked the trade very much. Mullin, contacted at home, did not share the sentiment.

"I wasn't happy at all," he says. "When things like that happen . . . I understand this is a business. That's cool. I still have to be selfish. That's my friend. I could care less about what this might mean for the team. I'm losing a friend, someone I see every day. My automatic sentiment is with the person, not the team. Is

he truthful? Is he honest? I don't care how it affects the team. I
didn't want Manute to go."

Business is business. Manute was back on the East coast.

His new friends in 1990 in Philadelphia with the Sixers were
teammates Charles Barkley and Rick Mahorn. This was a
change. Mullin was the quiet workman. Barkley and Mahorn
were compulsive comedians, making jokes about everything,
rolling through the schedule, simply taking the NBA celebrity life
as it came and treating it like a Marx Brothers plot. Barkley's
constant question was, "Do you believe we get paid for this
shit?" The games might be hard, but the life was the best. Barkley and Mahorn, both from poverty-level American back-
grounds, understood as well as any of the players in the league
that pressure was working a dull factory job and providing for a
family of six, not trying to convert a couple of foul shots. The
NBA was a temporary dream job, overpaid and wonderful, a
time to be savored.

Manute became a third in their group, a seven-foot-seven
straight man. He sometimes resembled the good kid, the quiet
kid from the front seats in the grammar school class who somehow had fallen in league with the rascals. He liked the rascals
and the rascals liked him.

"He's just a tall, skinny us," Barkley said. "No different. He
plays hard. He likes to have fun."

"You know the commercial you see on television about Africa,
Adopt a Kid?" Mahorn said. "We've adopted Manute."

A six-day road trip through the Midwest, stops at Milwaukee,
Cleveland, and Indianapolis, was a sampler of Manute's life with
the Sixers. All that was missing from making the trip a circus
parade was a calliope. Barkley told Manute that "maybe you're
big in your country, but this is America and here you're just
another tall guy." Mahorn said, "If it weren't for basketball

you'd be back home with a bone in your nose, just another sheepherder." They both expressed surprise that Manute's wife was pretty, because they figured she would be "one of those women we used to see on the cover of *National Geographic* in high school." Manute fired back.

"The problem with you black guys in America is that you do not have any tribes," he said. "You belong nowhere. You roll around the country. You are like loose balls on the court. That is what you are. Loose balls. When the referee says, 'Loose-ball foul,' do you turn around because you think he is talking about you? Think about it. Loose balls."

For Thanksgiving, Barkley and Mahorn had played a joke. Barkley told Manute he was taking him for an elegant holiday dinner. They went into a room where various dishes and silverware were laid out on a long table. Barkley removed the covers of a couple of dishes. Manute was interested. Barkley removed another cover. A hole had been cut in the table. Mahorn's head was through the hole and underneath the cover. Manute jumped back in shock. The trick was filmed and shown at halftime of a national game. Manute said he "almost turned white," and now was planning on revenge. He was not sure what he would do, but it would be something.

In Cleveland, less than an hour before the game, there was a typical scene. Barkley was stealing soap from the locker room shower, explaining that the savings would probably translate into a $3 beer in the hotel bar. Mahorn was eating from a tub of buttered popcorn. Manute had slowly gotten dressed in his uniform but was still wearing a pair of black street socks with little white polka dots on the side. The Sixers trainer asked him to come into the training room to have his ankles taped. Manute stood. Barkley decided it was time for *his* ankles to be taped.

One remark turned into another. Insult matched insult. Barkley put up his hands, prepared to fight. He went into a fine imitation of the Muhammad Ali shuffle. Manute put up his hands as if he were John L. Sullivan, preparing to defend his title against

Jake Kilrain. The two men circled each other. Less than an hour before the game.

"Rick," Barkley suddenly shouted, "he's messing with me again."

"I told you not to mess with my boy," Mahorn said, putting down his popcorn.

Together, Mahorn and Barkley attacked Manute. It should be noted that earlier they had taken assistant coach Fred Carter's top coat and 1930s-style felt hat from his locker. Barkley had worn the coat, Mahorn the hat. They had walked into the press room, where Carter was eating. "See this," Barkley announced before Carter and the other diners, "this is how you look when you wear these clothes, Fred." "Yeah," Mahorn said. "Like shit." Anyway, back to the fight. Mahorn grabbed Manute from behind. Barkley grabbed his ankles. Together, the two attackers lowered Manute to the floor. The other players watched. Manute struggled, hitting at Barkley with a New Balance sneaker. Mahorn proposed various tortures. Barkley suggested tickling Manute to death. It was a scene; the big man stretched so long across the floor. Finally, Barkley and Mahorn helped him to his feet, no easy process. Mahorn went back to the popcorn. Barkley let down his guard. Manute attacked. He put Barkley in a headlock, then lowered his head to touch Barkley's head. Barkley is bald. Manute has close-cut hair. The hair created a fine friction.

"Oh, not the hair," Barkley whined. "Rick, he's using the hair."

"You're on your own," Mahorn said.

All of this continued everywhere except on the court. In airports. In hotel lobbies. On buses. Everywhere. "Twenty-four hours," Manute said. "Including room service." Alliances might change, but jokes were constant. Barkley might introduce a friend in a Milwaukee restaurant. Manute would put the friend in a headlock and say, "Okay, Charlie, I have captured a white man. What do we do with him now?" Mahorn might be missing a shoe and find it in Manute's locker. How did it get there?

Manute might be missing a shoe. Okay, Rick, where's my shoe? Barkley might start everyone singing the "Theme from Shaft" at the Indianapolis luggage carousel, then move directly into the "Theme from the Beverly Hillbillies." Manute and Mahorn would sing along.

"You know what surprised me?" Barkley said in a serious moment. "I never knew Manute wanted to win so much. He wants to win as much as anyone I've ever seen in this league.

"A lot of people feel sorry for him, because he's so tall and awkward, but I'll tell you this: If everyone in the world was Manute Bol, it's a world I'd want to live in. He's smart. He watches CNN, all the news shows. He knows what's going on in a lot of subjects. He's not one of these basketball guys. Basketball's just one percent of it. You know what he was talking about the other day? Milk. He was saying that he grew up on milk straight from the cow. Squeezed it himself. Milk. He says, 'Charlie, what's this low-fat milk, two percent milk. Cows don't give us low-fat milk. We shouldn't drink it.' I don't know. Maybe he's got something."

Off the court, Manute was the biggest attraction on the team. On the court, his minutes were measured and he was a backup center, period. Barkley was the big star. Mahorn was a cranky bit player, taunting opponents and giving high fives to Barkley after someone had been leveled trying to drive to the basket. Manute was a curiosity, the ever-present buzz beginning when he came onto the floor, but a quiet factor in the game. Off the court, however, Manute was the one who stopped all pedestrian traffic. Not Barkley. Not Mahorn. The other players could stand at the side, at ease, as strangers asked to have their picture taken with Manute or simply stood and stared.

"You'd think they could get him on some steroids or something," a luggage handler said in Indianapolis. "You put a man that size on steroids, you'd have something."

"And I thought I had trouble buying clothes," a fat man said at a health club in Cleveland.

Two kids from upstate Wisconsin appeared at the game in Milwaukee and hung a bedsheet that read MANUTE FAN CLUB from the balcony. They said they had done this for three years, going only to the one or two games Manute played each year in the city. They said they weren't making fun, that they liked Manute a lot because he was "unique." In Cleveland, Manute wound up with the ball twice halfway between midcourt and the three-point line. The crowd yelled "Shoot" each time. He did not shoot. In Indianapolis, an older man behind the bench yelled mean things at Barkley for much of the game. Manute suddenly turned around and said, "Do you know that old men have heart attacks every day when they become excited? I would not be so excited if I were you." The man kept quiet.

Manute scored two points in the three games. He collected seven rebounds, blocked three shots. The Sixers were tromped in Milwaukee, 141–111. They were tromped again in Cleveland, 104–88. In Indianapolis, they rebounded with a 108–100 win. In celebration, Barkley and Manute went through a series of handshakes. Manute then bent down and rubbed heads with Barkley.

"I love to win, dude," Manute said. "I love to win."

A photographer from *Sports Illustrated* was on the trip to take pictures for an upcoming story about Manute. The photographer's search was for the perfect tall picture, a shot that would illustrate Manute's great height. Manute was not a willing subject. He would not allow the photographer to take a picture of him bending to shave or curled up on an undersized hotel bed. The photographer had to search. He seemed to follow Manute everywhere, dropping to his knees, even lying on his back to find a different angle. Nothing seemed exactly right. Then, Manute went swimming in the hotel pool in Cleveland. The picture that ran across two pages showed him stretched in the water, arms out, legs gently kicking. It was one of those pictures you can see and see again and never become tired of seeing. He looked like a giant surrealistic eel.

*   *   *

Life at home seemed to follow the same pace as life with Barkley and Mahorn. Atong gave the scene a certain stability, but Manute is not a person who likes quiet time alone. Back on the East Coast, with more people he knew, he was always surrounded by people, by friends, as many visitors as possible at any given time. Atong always seemed to be cooking and cleaning for a large crowd, not to mention the three children. The latest addition—almost three children in three years—was Chris, the son named after Mullin, Chalk, still the best friend. All of the children will probably grow to be tall, but Chris, the youngest, seemed to have the largest feet and hands as a baby.

"Chris is the one," Bill Sheehan, a family friend, says. "He's only a year old now, but you can just see he's going to be tall. Abouk, she's four, and already she's tall. I took her to a day camp that I run when she was about three and a half and she was the same size as kids who were six and seven. Madut is getting there, too."

Sheehan, now a parks and recreation director in Prince Georges County in Maryland, was in college and the next-door neighbor to the Ferrys when Manute arrived in Washington. In those earliest days, he was part of the support group. His mother used to wash Manute's clothes. He stayed as part of the daily operation, still fascinated by the things he sees and people he meets. He helped Atong become assimilated into American culture, almost filling the role of Chuck Douglas for her. He still helps. She does not drive, so he takes her on errands, writes out her grocery list, helps with the odd jobs.

"I'm ashamed to say that when all of this started, I didn't know anything about the world," he says. "I thought Africa was one country. That's how little I knew, growing up here and never thinking about anything else."

Manute would talk about the different countries he had seen in

Africa and the Middle East. He would describe the beauty of, say, Ethiopia. Ethiopia? Beautiful? Kuwait. Beautiful. Sheehan would invite him to family gatherings with his aunts and uncles for Easter or Mother's Day or other holidays. When Manute was married, Sheehan was at the airport.

"Atong was like Manute when he came here, she didn't know one word of English," Sheehan says. "She was very shy and very young. Only eighteen. Maybe less. It had to be tough for her. Then, she was pregnant almost right away, then pregnant again and again. It was hard for her to get out. She still hasn't made too many American friends because she's home so much. And Manute is traveling so much, it's been hard. But she's pretty good at English now and if you get to know her, get past the shyness, she's very funny. Just like him. She's just so busy all the time, so many people coming to the house."

Sheehan has simply tried to help. There always seemed to be another move to make, another appointment to keep at a doctor's office or dentist's office. He showed Atong American life. The kids rolled along, picking up the life naturally, cartoons on the television, toys on the floor. Abouk soon will be heading for nursery school and the other kids will follow. Natural. The return part of the deal was that Sheehan learned about Dinka life, African life. He sat with Manute and his Dinka friends as they got into animated arguments about events in the country. He went with the family during the summer to the house in Alexandria, to the Dinka colony in Nairobi, Kenya.

"You get to Alexandria with Manute and his house is like the Bol Hotel," Sheehan says. "All of these people come from everywhere. There's always something going on. It's not like anybody's free-loading or anything, it's just friendship. Everyone gets together to talk. To talk about the past. To tell stories. Everybody goes home at the end of the night, then ten o'clock in the morning it starts all over again. It's like this is the summer, but it's no vacation. It's the same thing as the season, only bigger. Manute is never alone.

"It's so different from the way we live. I got to thinking a lot about my family and my friends. My grandparents live in Lancaster, Pennsylvania. We get together on the occasions. On Christmas. Birthdays. Why don't we get together more? It's so natural with the African people. We have to make such a big deal out of everything. I decided I'd like to be closer to my own friends and family."

On the trip to Nairobi, Manute took great delight in pointing out the various animals and birds, the trees and the landscape. Wasn't this beautiful? Look. Sheehan remembers thinking that "this is his place." Manute said, alas, this was not true. He said they were close, but this was not home.

"I only wish I could take you to the south of Sudan," he said to his friend. "I only wish you could see."

"I really miss Manute," Chris Mullin says in the Ambassador Hotel in Barcelona. "He's one of those few people I know that whenever I see him, there won't be any pause in our relationship. It will be like we had just seen each other yesterday. Pick up just like that. Before I came over here, I was at my gym. I was walking out and the Roy Firestone show came on ESPN. Manute was the guest. I stopped right there. Just the sound of his voice. I watched the whole show. He was terrific."

Mullin has been thinking about friendship. He says the best part of the entire Dream Team experience is not all the notoriety or the $900 rooms or the endless buffets, it is the friendships that have been made. He has met these other players he has known only by their names and faces and tendencies to drive right or left, and shared experiences with them. His wife has met their wives. His baby has been in the same playpens with their babies. Isn't that more fun than all of this other stuff?

"I really miss seeing Abouk," he says. "I know my wife misses her, too. I want to see how much she's grown."

The opponent for the night is . . . who is it? Spain? Mullin thinks instead about people who are thousands of miles away. His wife comes across the lobby, carrying the baby. A picture is going to be taken in the game room/nursery. All the children of all the players. The Dream Team of twenty years from now.

"Remember when we took Abouk out on Halloween?" Mullin says. "How shy she was?"

Friends.

Happy as he was, the giant also wanted to go home. Some bad things had happened to his people and he wanted to see for himself. He had tried to help them and he would help some more. He wanted to see for himself. Were the animals gone? Was the land barren? Were the people hungry, starving, even dead? The giant went home.

And . . .

He cried.

The big C-130 can travel only one way on take-off from Lokichokio in northern Kenya. The runway is only a grass strip and at one end the grass is perpetually wet. The plane has to start in the wet and accelerate as fast as possible, hitting 130 miles per hour. The runway is short for a plane this size. The load on board must be under 160 tons and the speed must be 130 and that is when the plane can lift off the ground and into the air. With twenty yards to spare.

"You just want to close your eyes," Janet Green says. "The whole flight. Just close your eyes. You're carrying mostly grain, food. The grain is in these double sacks on these conveyors. When you reach the drop site, the plane has to go very low, maybe down to a hundred feet. The doors in the back are opened and you have very little time. You're so low. Everybody is just pushing like crazy, just throwing the stuff out. You want to get it out so you don't have to come this low again."

She is the Director for Education and Outreach for Oxfam America, an organization to combat world hunger, and she has been in the air above southern Sudan when the food is delivered to starving people and she has been on the ground with them, too, waiting. A nurse by training, she has worked in the hospital that is nothing but a warehouse for people, a building with a cement floor and numbers marked in chalk along the cinder-block walls. Each number designates a space for a sick person, who will sleep on a spread-out piece of cardboard. She has talked, in the light of day, with women and children who are embarrassed because they own no clothes and must stand naked, morning until night. She has dived into foxholes at the approach of planes that do not bring food—government planes. Will they be dropping bombs? Here?

She has ridden on roads that really aren't roads, a thirty-kilometer trip taking eight hours on a given day as drivers must sit and wait for a river to recede after a hard African rain. She has learned the different tribes, their different customs, talked with members of the Taposa, whose religious belief is that all of the cattle in the world belong to them, a gift from God, a position that can bring sudden conflict when the Taposa take cattle that other tribes have bred and raised. She has landed in bush planes on strips of dirt that have to be cleared first of giant anthills. She has found refugees from the war waiting for the plane, victims lying quietly minus an arm or both legs. She is not a saint. She is simply someone who wants to help, hooked by the things she has seen.

"My schooling in Vermont was as a nurse, so I guess that means I always wanted to help people somehow," she says in her Boston office, located in a grim building with iron bars on the windows to ward off intruders from a degenerating South End neighborhood. "When I moved here, I started volunteering for Oxfam. A job opened. One thing led to another. I was in the Sudan."

Her stories are told without pity. This is the way it is. The idea sometimes may develop from far away that life is cheaper in Africa, somehow different from here, but she has stood with the mothers whose children have died. She has seen the tears. Are they any different from tears in a hospital here? She thinks not, not at all. She helps raise funds here. She helps dispense the food over there. She never paid too much attention to basketball.

"Then I was driving one day with a man named Ashueil in Kapoeta," she says. "He is our agricultural coordinator in the village. We were talking. Women are usually treated differently in the Sudan, made to eat in another room, second-class citizens, not involved in conversations, but I am treated with respect because I am from so far away, I suppose, doing a man's job. I am an honorary man. That is the only way to describe it. They made me an honorary man. Anyway, we are driving and Ashueil—he speaks English—says he has a friend in the United States. I ask who that is. He says his boyhood friend is Manute Bol, who is a basketball player in the United States."

She knew of Manute mostly through things she had heard in the Sudan, the story of this man who had gone from the swamp to play in America, but did not know much about him. She and Ashueil talked on different days. Once, Ashueil pointed to a picture in the office. The picture showed a young boy wearing a loincloth. He was holding a thin stick and was surrounded by some small animals. Ashueil said that was how he had been. And Manute. That was how Manute had been. Ashueil asked a favor: If he wrote a letter to Manute, would she get it to him? There are no stamps, there is no post office in the south Sudan, along with no currency, no running water, no electricity, and no peace. She agreed.

From Boston, she eventually called Manute. She told him her name and described her organization and said that she had just returned from Sudan. He did not believe her. The Sudan? No Americans went to the Sudan.

"I was just in Kapoeta," she said.

"Kapoeta? You were in Kapoeta?"

"I was with Ashueil."

"Ashueil?"

A telephone friendship began. In his letter, Ashueil had written about his work with Oxfam and mentioned fund-raising efforts in America. He asked Manute to help. Manute was soon walking down the halls of Congress. Washington, D.C.

"Do you know how the ceilings are so tall, vaulted, in those Washington buildings, designed to show the insignificance of all of us against the government?" Janet Green says. "This is my first sight of Manute. He is walking through the halls of Congress and he must have been the first person who ever fit. The building seemed designed for him. Some of my friends were with him. They looked like children."

Manute had never been outwardly political, not in the early years in the United States. Deng was political; his father was a politician who was later killed in the civil war. Manute would talk politics with his Dinka friends and his American friends, decrying what was happening, but his public quotes mostly were as a humanist, or something like that. Why can't everybody get along? Why can't the Muslims in the north and the tribes in the south co-exist? He had been upset when the Muslim decrees of Nimeiri's government were issued and civil war began in 1983, further upset in 1985 when he was detained when he went home after his father's death. Nimeiri was deposed, however, and that had given him some hope. But the civil war continued. There was another coup early in 1989. More hope. But the civil war continued. Escalated.

It was raging now in 1991 and he was political. He was a man who could not go home. His last visit had been in the summer of 1989. He had gone to Khartoum with his family. The police took him to the station and detained him for a number of hours. He had always tried to help the starving and homeless in his country, raising money and supplies for the Sudan Relief and Rehabilitation Association, lending his name to their cause. He and his agent, Catapano, estimated that he had spent over $300,000 of his own money in trying to help the people of the Sudan. This was interpreted by the government as help for the rebels in the war. Manute said he was only trying to supply food to all people. People were starving. Not only that, the food was not going to his people. The government was diverting it, using food as a weapon. He was released, but told later that he should not return to the country. He would be in danger. That was why he had bought the house in Alexandria, Egypt. He could not go home. Alexandria was as close as he could be.

His sister was in Wau with her family and he could not talk to her. He owned the two houses in Khartoum, filled with his relatives, and he could not talk to them. He would try to call, try again, and always the connection to Khartoum or Wau would be made, then the phone would go dead. The government knew who was calling.

"You are going to Khartoum?" he said one day to a reporter, spelling out the sad existence of an expatriate. "I wish I could fit inside your suitcase."

Manute's political debut came at an event in Washington called the Hunger Banquet. It is Oxfam's biggest public relations event, part of a national day of "Fast for World Harvest . . . that others may eat." Similar events were being held in Hollywood, New York, and other major American cities. The gathered dignitaries were asked to draw straws to determine what their menu would be. Fifteen percent of the crowd would draw a straw of a certain color that would allow them to eat an elegant banquet, representing the wealthy of the world. Thirty percent would draw a straw that would entitle them to an average, middle-class meal. Fifty-five percent would draw a straw that would mean they would sit on the floor and eat only rice. This would demonstrate the inequality and the sheer happenstance of poverty and hunger. Who would be lucky? Who would not? The straws would decide.

Manute spoke. Assorted members of Congress and other high-rollers and schoolchildren from around the world were in attendance. Manute was nervous. He had taken the train from Philadelphia with Billy Sheehan. The Sixers held a special early practice to allow him to leave on time. What would he say? Billy Sheehan told him simply to speak from his heart. Didn't he know how he felt? He had said so enough times in casual discussion.

"If I were in the Sudan right now, I would be starving with the rest of my people," he said, standing in front of the group in his sportshirt and suit. "I eat good food here in America and I go to sleep at night and then when I wake up in the morning I see something on TV and feel really terrible. There's nothing I can do. I have about seventy of my people right now homeless in the capital of Sudan. They have no place to go."

He said his teammates had asked him why he was going through the bother, going to a dinner like this in the middle of the season. He said he told them his people had no food, no water, and were dying and needed help. He said he was hoping that the people of America would be compassionate, but he had friends who did not think Americans knew all that much about compassion. If they did, why would there be homeless right here? Why wouldn't somebody be helping these people? It was strong stuff, no George Bush syrup about "a thousand points of light." There were no speechwriters, no notes for this man who once did not know one word of English.

On the trip back to the train station, Manute was in a cab with Janet Green and Billy Sheehan. A homeless person approached the cab's window. He recognized Manute and asked for some change. Manute gave the man $20.

"Do you think I should have done that?" Manute asked when

the man left. "Maybe he will use the money for alcohol or drugs."

"You gave him something better than the money," Janet Green said. "You gave him yourself. You touched him. You have the power with your fame ... people meet you and they will remember it throughout their life. You gave him something to talk about forever. Yourself."

In the summer he went home for one day. That was all. One day in a nightmare. He was totally politicized now. He had met rebel leader John Garang during the season in Washington and was convinced about the cause. His last worries had been about his relatives, still living in the country, but now his relatives were dying anyway. The conditions had become worse and worse. Televised reports showed orphans burying other orphans who had died, children eating mice and rats. The Sudan was ranked third on the United Nations' misery index, behind only neighboring Somalia and Mozambique. Every day there seemed to be more reports of bombings and killings and of starvation at the refugee camps.

His trip was arranged through Garang's group, the Sudan People's Liberation Movement. The idea was to take footage of Manute and his people, to show the film on television in the United States somewhere, and to attract support and money and food. To try to stimulate a little outrage. Maybe a famous basketball player could make the average American and the American government notice what was happening. Maybe. Manute would try to edge this horror into the great televised jumble of sound bites and talking heads and make it meaningful.

He went first to Nairobi, where the trip would begin. If it began. There were problems. The only regular planes available into the south at the time were being flown by the Red Cross. The Red Cross would not take him. Too political. Another plane had to be found, another pilot. The pilot who eventually surfaced had a problem. His plane was spread in pieces across the hangar, being fixed. Manute had to wait. He sat in a $300-a-day room at the Nairobi Safari Club, next to the William Holden Suite. The Dinka of the area gathered. There was much beer, much conversation.

"It was fascinating to see him, talking in his native language, the change in his personality," says Tim Dwyer, a sportswriter from the *Philadelphia Inquirer* who was also making the trip. "He was so much more regal, so much more articulate. You realized how much, in America, he is still a fish out of water. I found myself sitting with all these Dinka, watching television. The news. A story came on from Milwaukee, about Jeffrey Dahmer. We're all watching. It was surreal. Here we are, in this land of starvation . . . and we're watching some guy in America who's eating people? It was surreal. I don't know what it all meant. It was just surreal."

Dwyer tried to clear up a few questions he had about Dinka life, Manute's life. Since all of the Dinka he met seemed to be related, he asked Manute how many uncles he had. "How do I know?" Manute replied. Dwyer asked how many cousins Manute had. "Too many to count," Manute replied. Dwyer finally asked why every other Dinka he met seemed to be named Deng. Manute asked why every other player in the NBA seemed to be named Johnson. A Nairobi newspaper ran a picture of Manute on the front page with the caption, "Manute Bol, tallest basketball player in the world. Plays for the Philadelphia 76ers, who poached him from the Washington Bullets. He makes $20 million per year." Dwyer asked if Manute had gotten a raise. Manute grunted.

The war dominated all conversation. Many of the visitors were soldiers taking a leave. One of the men had returned that day, reunited with his family for the first time in seven years. The entire region was a mess. Homelessness had become the natural state, families split apart, cattle destroyed, food gone. Some people were eating grass. The camp at Pochala, where Manute would go, now had a population of 130,000. Refugees who had gone to Ethiopia had been returned, fleeing strife in that country. There was a general wandering, a constant chance of bloodshed. The government had managed to split some of the tribes from the coalition under John Garang and now there were tribes killing other tribes. All of this was in a vacuum, nobody seeming to care outside the boundaries.

The United States, long a supporter of the military government in Khartoum through its many phases, now supported no one. The need for the Sudan as an ally against Soviet-backed Ethiopia had kept the United States tied to the dictators as late as 1989, quiet through all the massacres and famines so it would not embarrass an ally. There seemed to be a policy of benign neglect now. The Soviet Union was out of commission. The Muslims of Khartoum had backed Iraq in the war, so all of the West and most of the Middle East had turned against them. The turn was not far enough to embrace the rebels, however. The war was considered an intramural affair, no different from all of the other civil wars in the other hellholes of the continent. Attention was given elsewhere.

"This is what I do not understand," Manute said. "Why is the United States so concerned with all of these other places, with Eastern Europe and Kuwait and Peru, and not concerned about what is happening here? This is worse than what is happening anywhere."

The plane was eventually put together and took off, a week late. The pilot had to fly low and watch for the Soviet MiGs of the Sudanese Air Force. Manute, Dwyer, an *Inquirer* photographer, and a film cameraman and sound man were the passengers. The plane landed at the refugee camp in Pochala. The impressions were immediate. Overpowering.

"From the moment you step out of the plane your senses are assaulted by the armies of misery," Dwyer wrote in the lead to his story in the *Inquirer* Sunday magazine. "What's that smell? Rotting human waste and smoldering wet leaves, and, while you're sniffing, random flies are rocketing up your nostrils and lighting in your eyes. Only a moment has passed and balls of sweat are rolling down the small of your back as you try walking from the plane, which is a little dicey because a morning rain has turned the runway into cake batter. The air hangs like a wet towel and it takes all the energy you can muster to swat away the flies that are now swarming all over you, and suddenly your eyes adjust to the equatorial sunlight and you see thousands of people, standing before you, staring.

"They are more bones than flesh and they are dressed in rags or nothing at all and they are staring at you anxiously because you have just stepped out of an airplane and an airplane means to them one of two things: They will be either fed or bombed. And as they stand there waiting to see which it will be this time, a murmur rises among them as they realize this plane has brought neither food nor bombs, but a brother. Manute Bol unfolds his endless legs with the dignity of a great Dinka chief, ducks under a wing, and comes face-to-face with their naked despair . . ."

The sight to Manute was even worse than it was to a Philadelphia reporter. These were his people. This was how bad it was? He had known it was bad, but this bad? An old woman touched him and began to cry. She was from his village. Three tall men approached. He had played basketball with them, now they were thin and underfed, exhausted from a two-week walk from another refugee camp. Can this be? His people. He was taken on a four-hour tour of the camp, surrounded by children and adults, men and women, everyone touching him. He was as different from them—in his designer jeans and his nylon jacket and his big-time basketball shoes—as he had ever been from anyone in the United States. He came from a different planet. He came from a well-fed moon.

In the middle of the tour he met a man named Bol Nyuon. Manute did not expect this. Bol Nyuon was the best man at his wedding. Now he was here? Manute said his wife was not going to believe this. He did not believe this. The two men stood and stared at each other. There was nothing else they could do. There was no extra room on the plane, no papers, no escape. The feeling of helplessness was as thick as any of the smells. There was nothing to do.

"You want to help, but you can't," Dwyer says. "There is just so much to overcome. You want to take off your shirt and give it to someone, but that would only make everyone else sadder in his own situation. The scene I'll carry forever is this little kid, a boy, maybe four or five years old. He is naked and he is holding a little wooden plane with a red cross painted on the side. That is his only possession in the world. That little plane. He is holding on and won't let it go, ever."

The trip back to Nairobi was quiet. What could be said? The *Inquirer* photographer sat in the co-pilot's seat and tried to find landmarks on the map for the pilot. Manute slumped in his seat, in the back.

"I'm dead," Dwyer heard him say. "I feel dead."

Two days later, Manute flew to another refugee camp, this time a camp for Somalians on the Kenya border. The effects of the first trip obviously lingered. A public service announcement for C.A.R.E. was to be filmed by an NBA crew. The NBA hadn't wanted its people to go into the Sudan, afraid of the danger. Manute was still quiet, distracted.

"You could just see that he had been blown away," Jamie Most, of NBA Entertainment, says. "He was very disturbed, very discouraged. His attention span was minimal."

Three planes made the trip. Manute was on the last one. Most, arriving first, discovered that for a while he was the only white person in the camp, which was filled with thousands of people. He was an immediate celebrity, a curiosity, a subject of great interest. Some of the children had never seen a person with white skin. They alternately were pleased and terrified of him. They pointed. They laughed. Everywhere he went, Most felt eyes.

"It hit me, this is the way Manute has to live every day of his life," Most says. "I had never thought much about that. All of those people, staring at you all the time. Being so different. I didn't like it."

Manute went through the demands of the producers. These refugees were not his people. They did not know his language. They spoke Swahili; he did not know Swahili. There was the same suffering, though the danger was not as immediate. There was no chance of bombs. Many of the people did not know who he was, though they knew he was someone. They knew he was tall.

The commercial shows him handing out grain to a child, then walking with a group of people while an announcer says, "In his homeland of Africa, NBA star Manute Bol has shown that a little care can make a world of difference." None of the children, none of the people look like him. They are a lighter black, different features. Somalia.

"Show that you care," is the final message from Manute. He is not smiling. The Somalians are all around him. He is wearing a blue C.A.R.E. T-shirt.

He said his words. He went back to Nairobi.

"It must be so hard for Manute," Janet Green says. "He has to have such stamina. His reality is that so many of his people are suffering, so many of them are dead and yet he has this life and all of this money and there is nothing he can do."

Green was in Pochala two days after Manute left. She saw Ashueil and asked if he had seen Manute. Ashueil had missed him. The camp was so large, he was on one side and Manute was on another and they never saw each other. *In shala.* Another sad story in the Sudan. Another disappointment in a country of disappointments. When will life be easy and free again? Better?

"A woman came up to me at the camp," Janet Green says. "She had no clothes to wear and she was embarrassed. She still came up and said, 'I do not know who you are and I do not know where you came from, I only know that you have heard of my situation and have come to help me.' I thought about that later at night. At first, I guess I felt that I was something special, that the woman did not know who I was and where I came from, only that I knew the situation. I guess I felt superior. Then I realized that I did not know who she was or where she came from either. I was no different from her. We have such preconceptions, like someone would have all the answers. Nobody has all the answers. All we know is the situation."

The giant now lives in the Great Outside. In Philadelphia. And Washington. And Alexandria, Egypt. Philadelphia? He still does his tricks with the round ball and people still seem to like them well enough. He lives with his family. He has many, many, many friends. He thinks often of his home and that makes him sad, but he does the best he can. If he could do more, he would. He will see what happens next. How do these stories always end? He hopes this one is the same.

He will try to live . . .

It is a day after Palestine Liberation Organization leader Yasser Arafat's plane has disappeared in the Libyan desert. The reports are that Arafat was flying from Khartoum to Tripoli. Manute is interested. What was Arafat doing in Khartoum? Ask yourself. Manute has ideas, but he will not say what they are. He only says he does not hope Arafat is dead, does not hope anyone is dead, but that a certain fate was involved here. A warning.

"God has eyes," Manute says.

What does that mean?

"God can see what is happening."

A gold cross hangs from a gold chain against the front of

Manute's practice jersey. He is sitting on the floor at the St. Joseph's gym, his back against the rolled-up bleachers. Again, his size startles you. No matter how many times you have seen him, no matter how many stories you have heard, he will put himself in some situation that will make you look at his size all over again. In this situation, his legs are stretched across the floor while he talks, as if he were sitting under a tree. They run forever, his legs. Sometimes he crosses them, wrapping the right leg completely around the left, his right Reebok pump sneaker tucked on top of the left one. He has the look of a giant yoga master.

The season is dead. That is the sports story. Six games remain and the Sixers would have to win all six even to have a chance to make the playoffs. The Sixers are not going to do that. Everybody knows. This is April. The season will end on April 18 and Manute will be in the air within a week, flying to Cairo. His wife is already there. She has been in Cairo for most of the season with the three children, taking care of her mother, who has heart problems.

"Is she an elderly woman, your mother-in-law?" Manute is asked.

"Thirty-eight, thirty-nine," Manute says. "You must remember my wife is only twenty-three. She was eighteen when I married her."

The atmosphere around the team is the atmosphere of a junior high school class during the last week of the spring term. The grades are in and the books have been taken and the blackboards cleaned for the summer and nothing can be changed. The results might be terrible, but they are results. Done. There is no pressure anymore. Barkley is holding daily news conferences about being traded or about being treated unfairly or about anything at all. Talking. Talking. Talking. There is already speculation about the player draft. The Sixers will be in the lottery pool for the first time. There are rumors that Lynam might be fired. Who knows? It has been that kind of year.

Manute, along with everyone else, has not had a good season.

He has been a backup and there was a time, when Jeff Ruland came back to the team and was healthy, when Manute was not playing at all. The proposed offensive goal by Lynam—three baskets a game—was not reached. Not close. Manute averaged only 1.5 points and less than three rebounds per game. Once again, he scored fewer points per minute than anyone in the league. Once again, he did not score in double figures once. Once again, he played in more games—34 of 71—without scoring than any player in the league. He was a luxury player, a player who can be used only in certain situations, on a team that could afford few luxuries. When his team is ahead, Manute can enter a game and further confuse an already confused opponent. When his team trails, Manute is a liability. One-fifth of the offense is missing. The Sixers trailed often during the season. Manute sat.

He is still popular—a rumble beginning whenever he enters a game on the road, shouts of his name when he unfolds from the end of the bench at the Spectrum—but his limits are obvious. Barkley, in his as-told-to autobiography, said his "grandmother could score more points than Manute Bol." Barkley apologized, but was certainly right if his grandmother is any kind of a shooter. The price the Sixers paid for Manute, the first-round draft choice plus a player, again seems extravagant. Then again, the player was cut and the player the Warriors picked with the choice, Chris Gatling, has not exactly become an NBA All-Star. Then again, Manute's career has never really been based on points. It has been based on imagination.

"I have never been able to figure out the approach to the guy these NBA teams have had," says Webster, the coach at Bridgeport. "Why haven't they brought someone in to work with him? He was a pretty good shooter when he was with us, but it's disappeared. I saw a game in Golden State, his elbow was in the wrong shooting position, all over to the side. Why doesn't someone work with him? These teams spend all that money, why don't they hire some coach for $42,000 a year just to work with Manute? Wouldn't that be worth the money?"

"I don't think he's been used right since he went into the league," says Stacom, the USBL coach. "The coaches haven't had the right mindset. Even Nellie, and I love Nellie. Manute is outside the norm. Things have to be established just for him. I think coaches go too much with the stopwatches and the old traditional rules. It's like pro football. You're telling me that Rocket Ismail isn't worth the money he was asking in the NFL? He's only the most exciting football player I've ever seen in my life. What's he doing playing in Canada? It's a crime. You have to make changes for the exceptions to the rules."

"I would still like to see Manute with a good team," says Catapano, the agent. "It's ironic that Golden State would now be a very good team for him. Golden State wasn't good when he was there, everybody was too young, but now he would be a good addition for them. Philadelphia? I don't know. We shall see what happens in the off-season."

There is no worry about Manute's immediate future. He still has another $1.5 million guaranteed for the 1992–93 season, the final year of the contract. He also has instant options after that. Catapano says that teams always call from Europe, where he would be an immediate gate attraction and earn big money. He could play in Italy tomorrow for the same money he is making now. Probably more. The Harlem Globetrotters are an obvious option, too, if he wanted to live the barnstorming life for a year or two. He definitely will play an eighth NBA season, four years longer than the average league career lasts. He probably will play more.

"We were talking about him the other day," says Nelson, the Warriors coach. "He hasn't been playing in Philadelphia and we were wondering what we would do if he became available. What we decided was that we definitely would have to take a look. He is still interesting. He would help."

A box of new basketball jerseys is in Manute's locker. He ordered them long ago, with a picture of the Sudanese flag on the front and the words *New Sudan* underneath. The shirts are for a team he will form when he goes to Alexandria, a team filled with expatriate Dinkas. They will play a local schedule in the early summer against the St. Mark's Club, Zemalek, and any of the good teams around Cairo. Manute will be the center. The shirts, alas, seem too small. They all are "Large," nothing else. He needed "Extra Large." At least one. For sure. He does not know what to do.

"It's too late to take them back, I guess," he says. "I will take them with me."

He will spend his last few days in America gathering equipment and shoes and sporting apparel of all dimensions. This he will also take with him, eight suitcases filled for the trip, maybe one filled for him and his family, seven filled with gifts for other people. All his people.

"I will be back in Washington at the end of July," he says. "Start working out. In August, I will apply to become an American citizen. I want to do that. I will be both—American citizen and Sudanese citizen. I want to be a citizen of this country."

He wants to start a business some day, probably a restaurant. He has wanted to start a restaurant for a while, but Catapano has told him to wait until his career is finished. The thinking seems shrewd to Manute. Relying on someone else to run a business would be fatal. Wait. He is an intelligent man, quite intelligent. Everybody who has been associated with him says so. If he does not read very well, so be it. He has noticed that a lot of men who have not gone to college employ a lot of men who did. Arlene Bialic, his English teacher at Case Western Reserve, said from the beginning that Manute couldn't read, "but he sure could count."

The rest? It is all cloudy. The Sudan is always in his heart. His dream would be to live the modern, American way in the land where he grew up, to bring the conveniences of this world back to the people of the other world. He would have the ranch house and the satellite dish and the frost-free refrigerator and the microwave oven and his cows would graze outside. The neighborhood would be filled with his children and the children of his cousins and uncles. The language would be Dinka, with all of its clicks and clucks and the humor that he knew as a boy. He would switch to English when Chris and C.B. and Frank and Billy Sheehan and any of his American friends came to visit. He would keep a house in America, visit often, have his business. Both worlds.

It is an unrealistic dream, perhaps, but that is how dreams tend to be. He definitely wants to raise his children—and he wants many more children—in the Dinka tradition. He wants them to marry Dinka women and Dinka men. For the girls, he definitely expects a payment in cows. Why would he not? Should he be the fool, paying cows for the hand of Atong, then receive no cows when his own daughters are married? This is not a joke. He is serious. Dinka tradition. He does mention that he wants his children to go to school. His children now are from the educated branch of the Dinka family tree.

A sociologist of some kind might make a case that for all that has happened, the long trip Manute has taken through Khartoum and Cleveland, Bridgeport and the mechanized glitz of modern society, his life might have been best left alone. Is a man happier with the material goods of today or the spiritual goods of yesterday? A pastoral picture could be painted, Manute as a village elder now, telling his stories and revered by the people around him, a natural life so unlike the one he has to live in short pants in huge public arenas.

Manute would not buy this. First, the pastoral life has been destroyed by the carnage. His town no longer exists. Many of its people no longer exist. The cows are gone. The life, alas, is gone. As he said, he probably would be dead now. A tall man would be an easy military target. Second, success in basketball is what he wanted. Has anyone ever wanted it more, gone farther to get it? He was responding to the voice inside himself, not to anyone else. He was not captured in slavery and brought to a place he did not want to go, to do a job he did not want to do. This was what he wanted. He does not feel that anyone used him, ever. Other people might have tried to gain benefit from what he did, and some succeeded, but he also got benefits. And his benefits were larger than anyone else's.

"Really, so much, God has blessed me," he says. "I start to play basketball and God has blessed me."

He has regrets. He wishes that his father didn't die, that he was able to pay his father back with the reverence of a Dinka son once he found this job. He knows his father wanted him to live the other life, but he wishes he could show this life to his father now. He wishes. He wishes that his mother didn't die and that his sister was not so far away, that he could be with her and help. He wishes that all of the bad things did not happen in the Sudan. He wishes that he could help more. But what can he do? He is one man. He does the best he can.

"I would like to get more of my people over here," he says. "I try. I talk with everyone. The United States Immigration, they're really tough on me. I have been trying to get my sister out, but I cannot get a visa. Visas are so hard. I have a half-sister, she applied for a visa in Cairo. They told her there was no chance, that she should go back to the Sudan. What is that? I can't understand it. You see the ads on television. Sally Struthers. Sponsor a child in Africa. Okay, here I am. I want to get people out and I can't do it. I can't understand."

Some nice things have happened. He was talking about that the other night with a Dinka friend on the telephone. The basketball team at the Catholic Club, everyone dreaming about coming to America? Most of them have made it at one time or another. He has seen most of them here in his stops around the country. Dinka are always waiting for him wherever he goes. He now has an uncle who is a professor at the University of Miami, another who is a professor at Loyola-Marymount. He has a cousin who played last year at Oral Roberts. He estimates that as many as twenty Dinka were playing basketball in America last year. There was a big kid at Dayton, Shakor Mayok. Manute played with him back at Wau in the beginning. (No birth certificates, please.) There will be more big kids in the future.

The list of his new friends in his new country seems endless. Who has worked with him who has not liked him? It was interesting that when Magic Johnson, the Los Angeles Lakers superstar, held a press conference after his retirement because he had contracted the HIV virus, he mentioned that one of the first people who had called him was Manute Bol. He said he had never really known Manute, except as an opponent.

"People all have been nice in America," Manute says. "Bruce Webster. Kevin Mackey. Jimmy Lynam. Don Feeley. Ah . . . Don Feeley, he is the best. I wish there was something I could do for him. I will think of something. I love Don Feeley."

The crush of people can be a grind. The every-day attention. He has a built-in wariness with strangers and sometimes can be curt and rude, especially when presented with rudeness. He can also be warm and funny. His name alone can bring smiles to his friends. What was it that Sean Hood, the teammate at Cleveland State, said? "He has given us some great, cheap entertainment." He has been to more places in this country than most people who were born here. He has seen more sights, done more things. His cousin Akuei Mawal says Manute did not become just a basketball player in America, he became "a household name." Mawal says he tells friends that "only the superstars go to Arsenio Hall and David Letterman—Michael Jordan, Patrick Ewing, Manute Bol." The awkwardness and loneliness of Manute's arrival have been covered with a developed layer of sophistication. He has always been as confident of who he is and what he is as anyone could ever be. What did person after person say? He never slouches.

Seven feet seven.

"I am never bothered by the fact that I am tall," he says.

"When I was younger, I was bothered, but not now. My height is a gift from God. That is what I say. I did not create it. What would I do if my wife had five sets of twins? Would I throw some of them in the ocean because I did not want them? We take our gift. I do not say anything bad about someone who is short or someone who is fat. You have to live with what you are given.

"Who knows what God is dreaming for us? There is a reason. Look at what He has dreamed for me."

Manute and Barkley are now going for lunch. Manute is ready, standing in the locker room in a warm-up suit, holding his box of too-small New Sudan basketball shirts. Barkley is still talking with reporters. One of his comments in the last week was that he is "a Nineties Nigger." The comment made for good headlines. No one exactly is sure what he meant, but the reporters want more. Always more. Manute is waiting.

"Come on, Nineties," he says.

"Coming, Nootie," Barkley says.

They walk to the parking lot, the broad-shouldered American superstar and the ever-so-tall African. Barkley punches Manute on the arm. Manute puts down the box and strikes the John L. Sullivan pose. Barkley grabs a baby that a man seeking autographs is holding as some kind of offering. A baby? Barkley holds the baby in front of his face for protection. Manute unrolls a long arm, curling it around the baby, his hand slapping Barkley neatly upside the head.

Barkley returns the baby to its owner, signs a slip of paper, and heads to his car. Separate cars. Manute walks to a beige Mercedes 500SL. The car is his newest possession. He folds himself behind the wheel. This is a perfect final picture. Beige Mercedes. Seat back. Manute. He picks up a cellular phone and begins to dial.

During the season, a reporter from *USA Today* ranked bests

and worsts in the NBA. He called Manute the worst player in the league. He called Manute a joke, a travesty, and a lot of other unfavorable things. Barkley, the instigator, naturally not only gave the paper to Manute, but read the words. Manute was bothered.

"This article, it really bothers me," he said. "Am I the worst? I am not the worst. Can I be the worst? This bothered me for one day, two days. The third day, it doesn't bother me. I just say to myself, 'This man, he can go fuck himself.' "

. . . Happily ever after.

AFTERWORD

Jimmy Lynam was removed as coach of the Sixers at the end of the season and became the team's general manager. He was replaced as coach by Doug Moe. Charles Barkley was, indeed, traded, to the Phoenix Suns. He and Chris Mullin and the U.S. Dream Team won the Olympic gold medal.

Kevin Mackey coached the Fayetteville (North Carolina) Flyers to a second-place finish in the Global Basketball League and was looking for a position somewhere else in basketball. Cleveland State, playing at the Henry J. Gordon Arena and Convocation Center, a twenty-thousand-seat structure built with monies raised during the Mackey success, finished its basketball season at 16–13.

The University of Bridgeport qualified for the Division II Final Four but, alas, lost in the championship game to Virginia Union. Bruce Webster missed out on various coaching jobs, but his old job was saved when The Unification Church of Rev. Sun Yung

Moon purchased the university and indicated it would retain intercollegiate athletics.

One of the top teams in the still-functioning United States Basketball League was the Miami Tropics. The team was sponsored by the John Lucas New Spirit Treatment and Recovery Center in Houston and filled with recovering addicts.

Kevin Stacom stayed out of basketball, managing the Mudville Cafe in Newport. The restaurant is owned, in part, by Frank Catapano. Catapano did not represent one number one choice in the NBA draft, but was again dealing various free-agent hopefuls to various teams. Chuck Douglas was named assistant general manager with the Bullets.

There was no word from Tony Amin and none of the people interviewed in this book seemed interested in pursuing the basketball player named Dud. Manute said he knew Dud and that Dud was "too lazy to make it in the NBA."

The refugee camp in Kapoeta in the south of Sudan was overrun by government forces, the refugees fleeing to Kenya, to Lokichokio. Reports, as usual, were incomplete about the fighting. The government closed a large refugee camp on the edge of Khartoum, sending the people back to their original homes in the south. A *Life* magazine story entitled "Lost Boys of the Sudan" estimated that in the thirty-seven years of the two civil wars more than a million people have died. The story showed the plight of thousands of starving, homeless boys, gathered in bands for survival, moving around the countryside. One picture showed a boy holding three dead rats he had captured for dinner.

The dream of unbelievable, unbeatable basketball height persists. The following column appeared during the spring in the *Orlando Sentinel*. The headline was, "Is Eight-Foot Magic Center Just a Dream, Or What?" The writer was Brian Schmitz:

> The Orlando Magic have been preparing secretly to sign a nearly 8-foot-tall Dinka tribesman who is a distant cousin of Manute Bol, the 7-7 reserve center for the Philadelphia 76ers.

Magic GM Pat Williams declined to comment Tuesday on the imminent signing of Yad S. Looflirpa, who stands an incredible 7-11¼ and weighs 325 pounds. But sources requesting anonymity told the *Orlando Sentinel* of the interest by the club, which has been trying feverishly to arrange Yad's visa with the Sudanese consulate.

A source with the Magic said Yad was so impressive during private workouts in Motswania, Sudan, that Williams had feared other NBA clubs might catch wind of their find.

Interest in Looflirpa (Loo-FLUR-pa) has heightened after Stanley Roberts, the Magic's rookie center (7 feet) severely twisted his ankle. Roberts also becomes a restricted free agent after the season.

Williams sounded stunned and exasperated when this columnist contacted him at his home late Tuesday night. "How did you . . . there's nothing to this at all, I have no comment," he said.

Orlando's mystery player won't be unveiled until rookie and free-agent camp this summer.

The source said a party of Williams, Magic owner Rich De-Vos, injured forward Dennis Scott, and an African translator from the University of Central Florida flew to Motswania this month.

DeVos rented a warehouse and had a basketball goal installed. Scott and Williams worked on fundamentals with Yad for five days. A source said DeVos had to buy three more backboards in the Sudan after Looflirpa shattered the originals with dunks.

After the party left Motswania, DeVos hired two college basketball assistant coaches from Detroit and sent them to continue Looflirpa's instruction, the source said. DeVos, who could not be reached for comment, lives in Grand Rapids, Michigan.

Information about Looflirpa, which means "seer of clouds" in the Dinka language, is sketchy. Looflirpa, 27, is a Dinka priest who has been a virtual recluse the past 10 years, his only respite a game of "apunia," an African version of volleyball.

An orphan, he is fluent in five languages and has expressed an interest in settling in America and has followed Bol's career.

"Yaddy is further along than Manute was when he came here. He's heavier. Looks like a giant Karl Malone. He has better offensive skills than Manute. He's a good athlete, very coordinated, but he's not aggressive yet," the source said.

"He could be an ultimate intimidator and shot blocker. Pat's excited. Especially if we don't get Shaquille (O'Neal, LSU junior). I've seen a video of Yaddy and he's an awesome sight. Fans won't believe it."

Reached at his home in Orlando, Scott said, "I can't say anything. It's hush-hush."

The source said that Bol had been told by Looflirpa years ago not to inform any NBA officials about him. As a member of the Dinka tribe—the largest and tallest in Sudan—he wanted to avoid NBA scouts who had become familiar with Bol's shot-blocking ability.

Calls to Bol's home in Philadelphia were not returned.

"Yad had given his life to the priesthood, was a volunteer at a Job Corps Center, and had a nice farm. But after his stepfather passed away, he was alone," the source said. "He thought basketball might be a way to one day help the country's poor."

The source said it was actually Jill Williams, Pat's wife, who met Yad in Bol's hometown of Gogrial, Sudan, and informed Pat. She was there to check on the progress of a foster child the Williamses have been sponsoring. Pat and Jill have 14 children and all but four have been adopted from foreign countries.

Elat L. Lata of the Sudanese consulate sent a wire from Motswania only acknowledging that a "Mr. Looflirpa" had applied for a visa.

"They're trying to keep it under wraps," the source said. "But Yad's coming. We think he can catch on quickly. He's clever. The guy was his nation's spelling champion for years and plays a game where he can say words backwards. He's fun like Manute is. Give him a sentence or a name and he can say it backwards. That's how quick his mind works.

"Pat told him he didn't even want to try to say Looflirpa backwards."

The date the column appeared was April 1, 1992. A lot of Orlando residents missed the point. Local talk shows were filled with calls about "this Looflirpa guy." The *Sentinel* received a lot of mail. Schmitz found himself having to explain himself again and again.

"I thought I'd spelled it out pretty well that this was a fantasy," he says, "but I guess I didn't. People were just so eager to believe this idea, that there could be an unknown who was bigger and better than anyone else. People actually got mad when I told them it was a joke."

On June 24, the Magic selected Shaquille O'Neal with the top pick in the NBA draft. He is seven feet one. Big enough. He is twenty years old. His first salary request began with a long-term contract worth over $5 million per year.

Manute is back for another season with the Sixers.

For information on Oxfam America and its Sudanese relief efforts, write to:

Oxfam America
26 West Street
Boston, MA 02111-1206.